TECHNIQUES OF MONETARY CONTROL

TECHNIQUES
OF
MONETARY
CONTROL

BY JOSEPH ASCHHEIM

THE JOHNS HOPKINS PRESS: BALTIMORE

To the Memory of my Mother

SARAH PFEFFER ASCHHEIM

PREFACE

In recent years, monetary policy has been the subject of growing attention, concern, and study. Predominantly, it has been discussed in terms of its general effectiveness. Much less frequently has it been examined in terms of the comparative effectiveness of its different instruments. Yet the use of monetary policy is, after all, the application of *particular* tools of monetary policy. Hence, analysis of the general efficacy of monetary control must be founded upon examination of the comparative potency of different monetary-control techniques.

Thus, the present volume is a study of the scope and method of central banking in the framework of the contemporary monetary system of the United States. As such, the book is essentially a series of essays, each concerned with individual techniques of monetary control. The first chapter summarizes the conclusions of subsequent chapters, and explicates the general view of central banking that results from a synthesis of the book's principal conclusions.

Some parts of the volume, which have since been considerably modified, were first published in the *Journal of Finance, Journal of Political Economy, Economic Journal,* and *Southern Economic Journal.* I am indebted to their editors for generous permission to use these publications. I am also grateful to the Ford Foundation and to the Social Science Research Council for fellowships that were granted me in the course of my work on this volume.

I must further acknowledge the stimulation and encouragement that I have received from my present, as well as past, colleagues in the Department of Political Economy of The Johns Hopkins University, under the chairmanship of Professor G. Heberton Evans, Jr. To him, in particular, go my special thanks for many an hour of helpful discussion.

Last but also most, I am indebted to Professor Fritz Machlup, of Princeton University, and to Professor Richard A. Musgrave, of The Johns Hopkins University. Both made detailed comments and suggestions on the entire volume, and both took an active interest in its progress. This acknowledgment is but a small token of my appreciation of their valuable help.

Joseph Aschheim

Baltimore

CONTENTS

PREFACE, vii

CHAPTER 1 Innovations in Central-Banking Theory:
Review and Preview, 1

CHAPTER 2 Open-Market Operations Versus
Reserve-Requirement Variation, 19

CHAPTER 3 Supplementary Security-Reserve
Requirements, 33

CHAPTER 4 Open-Market Operations: "Bills-Only" Doctrine
and Economic Stabilization, 53

CHAPTER 5 Bank Rate, Rediscount Rate, and
Other Interest Rates, 83

CHAPTER 6 The Persuasiveness of Moral Suasion, 99

CHAPTER 7 The Contrast Between Commercial Banks
and Financial Intermediaries, 111

CHAPTER 8 The Control of Time Deposits, 135

INDEX, 155

TECHNIQUES OF MONETARY CONTROL

1

INNOVATIONS IN CENTRAL-

BANKING THEORY:

REVIEW AND PREVIEW

After a generation of depression, war, and postwar inflation, monetary policy in contemporary Western economies has been restored to an active role. This restoration, especially in the United States, has given impetus to renewed interest in the problems of central banking. In particular, attention has focused upon the implications for conventional monetary policy resulting from two widely noted developments. These are, first, the coming into existence of a large Government debt, and, second, the proliferation of financial institutions other than commercial banks.

With regard to these developments, the present volume examines the nature and efficacy of monetary control in terms of individual instruments, or techniques, of central banking. The institutional setting for the entire study is that of the contemporary monetary system in the United States. In various connections, however, comparison with other monetary systems is made, in order to illustrate the extent to which it seems possible to generalize from the American context to other monetary systems.

The purpose of this introductory chapter is to sketch the scope of the volume and to draw together the results of the succeeding chapters into an over-all view of the efficacy of monetary control. This over-all view is stated with due reference to the two differing interpretations of the efficacy of monetary control that are most prominent on the contemporary American scene.

The first of these interpretations, the so-called "availability" doctrine advanced by some key officials of the Federal Reserve System,[1] highlights the large size and wide dispersion of U. S. Government debt as a source of strength of the monetary authority. The second interpretation, "a theory of finance that encompasses the theory of money,"[2] characterizes the proliferation of financial institutions other than commercial banks as a source of weakness of an authority confined to monetary, as distinct from financial, control. The view of the efficacy of monetary control that results from the present volume coincides with neither of these interpretations, although it is substantially closer to the former than to the latter. Before these diverse conceptions of monetary control are considered, however, an outline of the principal elements of the present volume is in order.

I. SCOPE OF THIS STUDY

It has become a commonplace that conventional central banking includes these instruments: variation of cash-reserve requirements, open-market operations, rediscounting, and moral suasion. Accordingly, the nature and usefulness of each of these instru-

---

[1] See particularly Robert V. Rosa, "Interest Rates and the Central Bank," in *Money, Trade, and Economic Growth,* in honor of John H. Williams (New York: The Macmillan Company, 1951), pp. 270-295; and, for various other references, Assar Lindbeck, *The "New" Theory of Credit Control in the United States: An Interpretation and Elaboration* (Stockholm: Almqvist & Wiksell, 1959).

[2] John G. Gurley and Edward S. Shaw, *Money in a Theory of Finance* (Washington, D. C.: The Brookings Institution, 1960).

ments is examined in ensuing chapters. Three further problems of central-bank technique are also considered: secondary reserve requirements, the position of financial intermediaries versus that of commercial banks, and the control of time deposits at commercial banks. Following the sequence of their treatment in succeeding chapters, let us take up, in turn, each of the indicated subjects.

(i) The variation of cash-reserve requirements permits the central bank to reduce or expand the volume of member banks' excess cash reserves by a stroke of the pen without having to resort to the open market, to changes of the terms on which it lends to member banks, or to efforts at persuasion of private enterprises. Furthermore, of the four instruments of conventional monetary control only two, the variation of reserve requirements and open-market operations, enable the central bank to absorb or release cash reserves entirely on its own initiative. Consequently, the variation of cash-reserve requirements is usually analyzed by means of a comparison with open-market operations.

Considering the two techniques on such a comparative basis, we find that the variation of cash-reserve requirements is, in general, inferior to open-market operations as a means of central-bank control. In the case of a restrictive monetary policy, i.e., under conditions of excess demand for private credit, there is an asymmetry between the two central-bank instruments that militates against reserve-requirement variation. The asymmetry is that greater shifting from Government securities into private loans is induced by an increase in reserve requirements than by restrictive open-market operations. In the case of an expansionary monetary policy, i.e., under conditions of substantial excess cash reserves, there is also an asymmetry between the two central-bank instruments that militates against reserve-requirement variation. Here the asymmetry is that greater shifting from excess reserves into private loans is induced by expansionary open-market operations than by a reduction in reserve requirements. Thus, whatever merit there may be in endowing the central bank with the tool of reserve-requirement variation, open-market operations are a superior instrument for contra-cyclical monetary policy.

(ii) Imposition of a supplementary security-reserve requirement permits the central bank to "insulate" from the open market that portion of Government debt that member banks must hold to satisfy the supplementary requirement. Hence such a technique of central banking, now in existence in several countries but not in the United States, prevents the bank from switching out of the required securities into private loans even when the incentive for switching is present. Here, then, would appear to be a useful device for curbing the extension of private credit by member banks that unload Government securities in response to an upsurge in the demand for private loans. Applying, however, some propositions similar to those we use in connection with the variation of cash-reserve requirements, we obtain a conclusion that belies the seeming usefulness of a supplementary requirement.

The conclusion is that if supplementary requirements are to be imposed as part of a restrictive monetary policy, i.e., at a time of excess demand in the private credit market, they must absorb the bulk of bank-held Government debt. Otherwise, they will stimulate more bank switching out of freely disposable Government securities into private loans than would occur in the absence of the requirements. Furthermore, the use of supplementary security-reserve requirements as an insulation device implies deviation from the principle underlying the institutional separation of Treasury from central bank. Even if one favors movement toward abandonment of this principle, it does not follow that supplementary security-reserve requirements, subject only to infrequent or rare variation and thus administratively feasible, would therefore be desirable. The question of desirability reduces to a choice between supplementary security-reserve requirements, on the one hand, and higher cash-reserve requirements, on the other. Higher cash-reserve requirements not only avoid the practice of forced lending to the Treasury by certain private institutions, but also permit a greater reduction in the interest burden of Government debt than that afforded by comparable security requirements.

(iii) The technique of open-market operations has three distinct, though related, aspects: first, the absorption or release of member-bank reserves; second, the influencing of the level of interest rates; and, third, the influencing of the structure of interest rates. Thus an open-market operation absorbing or releasing reserves of a given amount may be conducted in a variety of ways, each of which will have a different influence on the structure, as well as the level, of interest rates. For example, a given change of member-bank reserves can be brought about by an open-market operation that is confined to the short-term sector, or that is confined to the long-term sector, or that is made to include both sectors. On the other hand, an open-market operation may be conducted so as to alter the structure of interest rates without, on balance, absorbing or releasing member-bank reserves. For example, the central bank may sell a given amount of short-term securities while simultaneously buying an equal amount of intermediate-term and long-term securities.

Should the central bank change the volume of member-bank reserves by confining its open-market operations to one particular sector? Should the central bank engage in open-market operations that are designed to effect no change in member-bank reserves but only in interest rates? If rules are to be formulated in response to these two questions, under what circumstances should exceptions to such rules be allowed?

The foregoing and related questions have been much discussed in the United States in connection with the Federal Open Market Committee's policy of confining System open-market operations to the short-term sector except in the case of acknowledged "disorderly" market conditions. Accordingly, we explore the technique of open-market operations in terms of the implications of the Federal Reserve's "bills-only" policy. We do so from two points of view: that of the theory of the term structure of interest rates, and that of actual Federal Reserve experience with operations in pursuit of its policy.

The results of this exploration diverge from the "bills-only" doctrine. A review of the principal theories of interest-rate structure indicates that they have one conclusion in common. The conclusion is that there are variations in the rapidity of transmission of changes in general credit conditions among the markets for debt instruments of different maturities. Accordingly, there may, at times, be unresponsiveness of long-term interest rates to open-market operations confined to short-term instruments. In consequence, a central bank that is endowed with the capacity to operate in any maturity sector of its choice is clearly not helpless in the face of unresponsiveness of long-term rates to changes in short-term rates. Such unresponsiveness can be overcome by directly operating in the long-term sector.

Now when the lack of response of long-term rates to a decline in short-term rates occurs in the course of a recession, abstention from open-market operations in the long-term sector impedes the effectiveness of monetary policy by letting a decline in economic activity deepen. To defer operation in the intermediate-term and long-term markets until such time as there emerges what the Federal Reserve acknowledges as an actual disorderly market condition may, in the case of a sizable business downturn, be tantamount to locking the barn door after the horse has been stolen.

This last inference is corroborated by our consideration of the conduct of open-market operations in the recession months of the first half of 1958, preceding the crisis-like behavior of the Government securities market in July of that year. In those months of the severest recession in the postwar American economy to date, adherence to the "bills-only" doctrine contributed to the development of a maturity structure of interest rates that was clearly inconsistent with the objective of economic stabilization. Thus, on empirical—as well as theoretical—grounds, the central bank can ill afford to renounce its potential influence over the structure of interest rates by confining its open-market operations to the short-term sector.

(iv) Rediscounting by the central bank is an instrument of monetary control whose use has been at the very foundation of both the theory and the practice of central banking. Linked with the history of the Bank of England, the initiation of rediscounting by that institution rendered it a lender of last resort—the classic hallmark of central banking. And to the present day, the Bank of England's Bank Rate remains a conspicuous tool of British central banking. In the United States, as well, establishment of the Federal Reserve System is bound up with the institution of rediscounting by the twelve constituent Federal Reserve Banks. Though not as important an instrument as it once was, rediscounting has staged a remarkable comeback in the practice of American central banking since the restoration of monetary policy to an active role through the Treasury-Federal Reserve Accord of 1951.

We examine the nature and functions of rediscounting by comparing its American and English uses. This comparison sheds light on the extent of influence of institutional differences upon the character of particular tools of monetary control. In addition, this comparison leads us to a critical appraisal of the rediscounting instrument in its recently revived American version.

On the basis of our comparative analysis, we arrive at the conclusion that discretionary rediscounting in a monetary system with an extensive Government securities market is primarily a mechanism of escape from the impact of monetary restraint. Thus, in the specific case of contemporary American central banking, the rediscount facility has not served the cause of the central bank either as lender of last resort, or as moderator of cyclical fluctuations, or as promoter of the development of the money market. The constructive proposal to which this critical appraisal impels us is for abolition of the existing rediscount facility and its replacement with nondiscretionary, penalty-rate rediscounting. The penalty rate would vary automatically in correspondence with the Federal-funds rate, which would be rendered more flexible than it is at present.

(v) Moral suasion is the subtlest and, hence, the most elusive of the tools of conventional central banking. Loosely interpreted, it is well-nigh universal in application, being simply the exposition by the monetary authority of the rationale for its actions. Strictly and more commonly interpreted, moral suasion is the exercise of verbal pressure, through direct communication, by the monetary authority upon particular financial institutions. It is to the feasibility and desirability of moral suasion as strictly interpreted that the greater part of our attention is devoted.

Thus, on the basis of the experience of several central banks, we explore and illustrate the principal factors in the feasibility of moral suasion. The presence or absence of any of those factors differs widely in consequence of certain institutional features that vary greatly with time and place.

Yet wide differences in the presence or absence of factors in the feasibility of moral suasion do not mean that all generalization about the desirability of this instrument is impossible. On the contrary, we find—as we do in the case of each of the other techniques of monetary control—that our inquiry leads to an operationally meaningful generalization about the desirability of moral suasion. Specifically, if the central bank has the capacity to engage in open-market operations in the framework of an extensive Government securities market, moral suasion is superfluous. Our generalization notwithstanding, moral suasion continues to be practiced by the monetary authorities in the United States even though they are endowed with the tool of open-market operations in the context of an extensive Government securities market. This fact, as our discussion highlights, is a result of failure by the Federal Reserve System fully to utilize the tool of open-market operations.

(vi) The position of commercial banks in relation to that of other financial institutions has, in recent years, been the subject of much attention and discussion. Are commercial banks but one of several variants of financial intermediaries? Has the efficacy of conventional techniques of central banking been weakened by the proliferation of financial intermediaries? Should the monetary authority extend its direct regulatory activity to encompass not only commercial banks but all financial institutions?

Response to these questions entails empirical, theoretical, and policy considerations. We set forth these three sets of considerations with reference to the American financial system over the past few decades.

On the empirical side, the claim of commercial-bank retrogression relative to other financial institutions appears misleading on several counts. Particularly noteworthy is the disregard of the diverse behavior of demand deposits and time deposits in the course of commercial-bank development since 1929.

On the theoretical side, the conceptual dichotomy between commercial banks as creators of loanable funds and financial intermediaries as brokers of loanable funds is seen to withstand recent counterarguments. This dichotomy follows from the money-creating ability of commercial banks due to their demand-deposit operations under a fractional-reserve system.

On the policy level, conventional central banking appears strengthened, rather than weakened, by the vastly expanded scope for the tool of open-market operations. By virtue of this instrument, the monetary authority has been brought into direct interaction not only with commercial banks but with financial institutions generally. And in light of the aforementioned theoretical and empirical facets of the contrast between commercial banks and financial intermediaries, a suggested policy reform—to which we devote the concluding chapter—is that the time-deposit operations of commercial banks be freed from central-bank regulation.

(vii) In the United States, central-bank regulation of the time-deposit operations of commercial banks includes the setting of a minimum cash-reserve requirement and a maximum limit on interest rates payable to depositors. We examine the case for continuation of these regulatory techniques in terms of the principal arguments that have been put forward in their support. Though couched in the American setting, our examination of these arguments is of relevance to other monetary systems as well.

We find that, in the case of the United States, none of the arguments in question has remained sustainable. In other words, the two regulatory techniques noted above have become outdated as a result of clarification of the economic difference between demand deposits and time deposits.

The first argument considered is that time deposits are money and, therefore, must be subject to central-bank control. Upon scrutiny, this contention turns out to be no more than a subterfuge for defining away the problem.

Second under scrutiny is the argument that commercial banks would have incentive to induce customers to shift deposits from the demand to the time category, in the absence of a minimum cash-reserve requirement and of maximum permissible interest rates applicable to time deposits. This allegation is shown to be both internally inconsistent and erroneously generalizing from past conditions in which the monetary authority lacked adequate control over the *demand*-deposit operations of commercial banks.

Third to be reviewed is the contention that the proper criterion for distinguishing among commerical-bank deposits is not formal classification into demand and time categories but actual rate of deposit turnover. We find that not only would a reserve requirement entirely based on velocity amount to a triviality in the case of what are now time deposits, but that the present formal classification has—at least since 1933—come to mean the difference between money and other financial claims.

Finally, we examine the argument that if vault cash is counted as part of required reserves against demand deposits, the complete exemption of time deposits from a reserve requirement would constitute discrimination against member banks with a high ratio of time to demand deposits. This suggestion turns out to be superfluous under a system which, in recognition of the nonmonetary character of time deposits, segregates the assets held against time-deposit liabilities from assets held against demand-deposit liabilities.

II. EFFICACY OF MONETARY CONTROL

From these studies, as outlined in the preceding section, there emerges a general view of monetary control that is distinguishable by two basic propositions. First, in the context of an extensive Government securities market, the tool of open-market operations imparts efficacy to monetary policy not only with respect to the volume of bank reserves but also with respect to the term structure of interest rates. Second, this dual efficacy of monetary policy is consistent with and uncompromised by the institutional limitation of direct central-bank regulation to commercial banks. Let us explore further each of these propositions.

(i) A marketable Government debt of significant size and dispersion enables the central bank to do substantially more than merely to vary flexibly the volume of member-bank reserves. Such a debt enables the central bank, at its own initiative, to influence interest rates throughout the gamut of money and capital markets. This active influence can be exerted with or without simultaneously varying the volume of member-bank reserves. Here then is an instrument whereby the central bank can come into direct contact with the state of supply and demand in all the maturity sectors of the market for loanable funds. Such contact is here accomplished not by means of direct regulation of the operations of thousands of individual institutions but rather by means of the open market in which these institutions take part.

No other technique of central banking—indeed, not even all the other techniques of central banking taken together—can approximate the instrument of open-market operations in terms of the efficacy imparted to the monetary authority. Thus, the variation of cash-reserve requirements can, at best, serve only the purpose of changing the volume of member banks' excess cash reserves; it cannot serve the purpose of influencing particular maturity sectors of the loanable-funds market. Rediscounting can at best absorb or release bank reserves by putting the central bank in direct contact with the short-term sector; it does not endow the central bank with the capacity to influence directly the structure of interest rates at other points than the short end. And moral suasion is, at best, a means of substituting words for actions; it is no safeguard against the perennially possible failure of words to effect the central bank's wishes.

As concluded in this study, the technique of varying cash-reserve requirements for contra-cyclical purposes, the technique of nonpenal, discretionary rediscounting, and the technique of moral suasion can all be dispensed with if full use is made of open-market operations. A policy of confining open-market operations to one particular sector, as under the Federal Reserve's "bills-only" doctrine, constitutes an obstruction to open-market operations that are intended to influence the structure of interest rates. This confining policy, and the continued use of nonpenal, discretionary rediscounting, have been pursued by the Federal Reserve within the framework of the so-called "availability" doctrine of credit control in the United States. We must, therefore, turn our attention to this theory.

As previously indicated, the "availability" doctrine highlights the size and dispersion of public debt as a source of strength for monetary policy. Moreover it emphasizes the direct effects of monetary policy upon the behavior of lenders rather than upon the behavior of borrowers, savers, and investors; and it suggests that a change in the "availability" of loanable funds is a more important influence upon spending than is a change of interest rates. Accordingly, the central bank can potently influence the availability of credit even if it brings about only modest fluctuations of interest rates. Thus, yield changes of, say, ⅛ of 1 per cent for long-term bonds, in combination with changes in the availability of credit, can have significant market effects. Hence, monetary policy can make its contribution to economic stabilization to the tune of minor variations in interest rates.

The "availability" doctrine goes on to argue that because of the enormous wartime growth in the proportion of Government debt to total debt at all maturities, "there is no longer any impediment to a substantial flow of resources back and forth between the short-term and long-term markets."[3] Therefore, it has become realistic to expect a synchronous movement of interest rates on comparable debt instruments of all maturities. The explanation for this claim is that

> Clearly, through the medium of government securities and the lengthened term distribution of "bankable" private debt, a real fluidity is imparted to movements between the short-term and long-term markets. And while it may generally be expected that longer-term yields will not shift as swiftly as the shorter-terms in response to changes in credit availability associated with day-to-day variations in the economic outlook, the long-term market will definitely be influenced by any sustained ease or tightening in the short-term market.[4]

In view of such express confidence in the transmissibility of sustained pressure from the short-term to the long-term sector, the Federal Reserve System's espousal of the "bills-only" policy harmonizes with the "availability" doctrine.[5]

As there has accumulated an abundance of criticisms of the "availability" doctrine, no full-scale critique of the doctrine will

[3] Rosa, *op. cit.*, p. 281.

[4] *Ibid.*

[5] It may be mentioned, however, that some leading exponents of the availability doctrine have subsequently dissented from the "bills-only" policy. Presumably, they would favor corresponding modifications in their formulation of the "availability" doctrine.

here be attempted.[6] Rather, we shall confine ourselves to the points of difference between this doctrine and the general view of monetary control to which this study leads.

As the above outline of our analysis of the "bills-only" policy brings out, neither the theory nor the actual behavior of the interest-rate structure supports the claim that there is regularity in the transmission of sustained pressure from the short-term to the long-term market for debt instruments. In the case of the "availability" doctrine, the claim of the existence of such regularity is a result of unwarranted generalization in two respects.

First, the "availability" doctrine includes too hasty a generalization on the basis of the extraordinary fluidity of funds between short-term and long-term Government securities that characterized the period of the price-support policy of the Federal Reserve during and immediately after World War II. It was certainly correct to point out in 1950 that "switches [between the short-term and long-term markets], compounded of judgments concerning both the economic situation and the market intention of the System authorities, have not only become a commonplace, they have actually degenerated into a disruptive 'playing the pattern of rates' on several occasions during and following World War II."[7] It was, however, incorrect to infer directly from the fluidity of funds that inevitably characterized the period of the price-support policy to conditions under which the Federal Reserve would be free, as it has been since 1951, to back away from the Government securities market at its own discretion. Commitment to support given levels of Government security prices rendered all such securities perfectly interchangeable with each other and with money. But this was a special case: once the support policy was abandoned, perfect interchangeability ceased.

---

6 See Lindbeck, *op. cit.*, for one such critique and for references to others.

7 Rosa, *op. cit.*, p. 281.

Second, the availability doctrine was conceived in the conviction that the looming danger to economic stability is inflation rather than deflation. Now, as our ensuing analysis of the "bills-only" policy suggests, there is some basis for expecting that in times of inflationary pressures the fluidity of funds between the different maturity sectors heightens. But here again we are dealing with a special case: inflation. The general case is the entire business cycle; and, as we have already emphasized, there is no uniformity throughout the business cycle in the responsiveness with which impulses are transmitted from the short-term to the long-term sector.

Once we recognize the possibility of unresponsiveness in the transmission of pressures from one maturity sector to another, the "availability" doctrine's assertion of the adequacy of modest interest-rate fluctuations is seen to be an overstatement. Indeed, the overstatement becomes all the more pronounced under the impact of the "bills-only" policy: if the monetary authority confines its open-market operations to the short-term sector even when the long-term sector is unresponsive, greater variations of short-term rates will have to be contemplated than in the case of direct operations in the long-term sector. In other words, if one objective is moderation of interest-rate movements, the "bills-only" policy is a palpable barrier to its attainment. Moderation of interest-rate movements is most efficiently served by an open-market policy that is not constrained to a single maturity sector as a means of influencing all other maturity sectors.

In regard to rediscounting, the "availability" doctrine attaches secondary yet considerable significance to variation of the Federal Reserve's discount rate as a direct influence upon the cost of commercial-bank credit and as a psychological signal of a change in central-bank policy and in the state of the economy. In view of our detailed inquiry into the rediscount facility in Chapter 5, suffice it here to note that both for influencing the cost of bank credit and for signaling a change in monetary affairs, open-market operations are a more flexible and accurate instrument than periodic alterations of the discount rate.

Yet one important element in the availability doctrine is fully embraced in the view of monetary policy that emerges from our analysis. That element is the ascendency of open-market operations among the different techniques of monetary control in the context of an extensive Government securities market. Far above all other techniques, open-market operations "bring the central bank into contact not only with the volume of available bank reserves, but also with the portfolios of all classes of lenders."[8] It is to the lasting credit of the "availability" doctrine that it has been a stimulating contribution to recognition of the function that a large and widely distributed government debt enables the central bank to perform in the quest for economic stability.

(ii) Direct central-bank regulation of commercial banks is founded upon acknowledgment of the capacity of commercial banks to create money. With respect to the money-creating capacity, commercial banks are unique among all private financial institutions. This uniqueness is due to the fact that among all the types of deposit liability of private financial institutions, only demand deposits are widely accepted as means of payment. Hence, for the purpose of limiting their unique money-creating capacity, commercial banks are the object of direct central-bank regulation.

Not having the capacity to create money, private financial institutions other than commercial banks are financial brokers or intermediaries in the sense that their lending and investment activity is limited to whatever volume of funds spending units place at their disposal. Hence, the central bank's ability to limit the supply of means of payment as it sees fit is in no wise compromised by the confinement of its direct regulatory activity to commercial banks. For as creators of money, commercial banks are without competitors in the private financial sector: the central bank that controls the demand-deposit operations of com-

[8] *Ibid.*, p. 280.

mercial banks, as well as the issue of currency, controls the supply of the circulating medium.

As previously emphasized, however, control over the supply of money is but one dimension of central-bank activity in an advanced monetary system such as that of the United States. The other dimension is the whole gamut of interest rates that the size and dispersion of Government debt enable the central bank to influence. But the exertion of this influence is also uncompromised by the confinement of direct central-bank regulation to commercial banks. For open-market operations can reach out to all open-market participants, including not only commercial banks but the entire financial sector.

Yet in recent years a broad challenge has been posed to the limiting of direct central-bank regulation to commercial banks. This challenge is based upon the previously mentioned new "theory of finance that encompasses the theory of money." As Chapter 7 is devoted to the subject of commercial banks versus financial intermediaries, we shall here only briefly summarize the essence of the new theoretical approach at issue and our treatment of it.

The new theory of finance is opposed to the notion of a fundamental dichotomy between commercial banks and other private financial institutions. It does acknowledge that the monetary system "is unique in being the administrator of the payments mechanism."[9] It considers, however, all financial institutions as similar in other respects. Thus, in its revised and definitive version, the new theory holds that the monetary system and other financial institutions alike can all increase the supply of loanable funds.[10] The creation of loanable funds, is therefore, not the exclusive prerogative of spending units or of spending units and the monetary system alone. All financial institutions can exercise this prerogative.

[9] Gurley and Shaw, *op. cit.*, p. 243.
[10] *Ibid.*, pp. 218-221, 243.

But is it consistent, on the one hand, to regard the monetary system as unique in being the administrator of the payments mechanism and, on the other hand, to consider all financial institutions as able to create loanable funds? The uniqueness of the monetary system derives from the fact that, among all financial institutions, only its deposit liabilities are widely accepted as means of payment. Hence, to grant this uniqueness of the monetary system is to grant that other financial institutions are unable to engage in the net creation of money: their deposit liabilities are not widely accepted as means of payment. Not being spending units and not having the capacity to engage in the net creation of means of payment, financial institutions other than the monetary system are loanable-funds brokers exclusively. This fundamental distinction between the monetary system and other financial institutions is a logical basis for the focusing of direct central-bank regulation upon commercial banks.

2

OPEN-MARKET OPERATIONS

VERSUS RESERVE-REQUIREMENT

VARIATION

I. THE ISSUE

Widely divergent conclusions have been reached in regard to the proper choice between open-market operations, on the one hand, and variation of cash-reserve requirements, on the other. Whereas several scholars have suggested increases of reserve requirements as an alternative or supplement to counter-inflationary open-market operations, central banking authorities, as well as commercial banking circles, are generally opposed to such an innovation.

Thus, in comparing the short-period application of the two instruments, one writer considers it "a fact that if restriction of the deposit total [of commercial banks to a particular level] is thought right by the central bank, its enforcement by one weapon is merely a substitute for enforcement by another."[1] Accordingly he adjudges as lacking in substance "the bankers' dislike of the reserve variation weapon . . . when this weapon is confined to short-period service as an alternative to open-mar-

[1] Richard S. Sayers, *Central Banking After Bagehot* (Oxford: Clarendon Press, 1957), p. 89.

ket operations."[2] His reason for this view is that, "on the assumption that the central bank achieves equal success in its attempts to regulate the liquidity of the economy, the profitability of banking is unaffected by the choice between variation of reserve ratios and open-market operations."[3]

By contrast, the Chairman of the Board of Governors of the United States Federal Reserve System states that,

> The reserve-requirement instrument is not interchangeable with the open-market instrument. Unlike open-market operations, the results affect immediately and simultaneously all banks. . . . Changes in requirements, moreover, cannot be made frequently—especially on the up side—without unduly disturbing the operations of individual banks. . . . Changes in reserve requirements are, therefore, made infrequently and typically involve a fairly sizable volume of funds. The effects tend to be large and concentrated within a short period of time. The instrument is more appropriate for making a major change in the volume of available bank reserves than it is for short-run adjustments. It is not adaptable to affecting bank reserve positions on a day-to-day and week-to-week basis, as are open-market operations. . . . In fact, it may be desirable to engage in partially offsetting open-market actions in order to cushion the impact of reserve requirement changes in credit markets.[4]

In general accord with this reasoning, other writers have recurrently argued that changes in reserve requirements could be made by much smaller degrees than hitherto, correspondingly reducing the resultant shock effect upon the commercial banking system.[5] Additionally, it has been suggested that the immedi-

[2] *Ibid.*, p. 90.

[3] *Ibid.*, p. 89.

[4] Replies of the Chairman of the Board of Governors of the Federal Reserve System in United States Congress, Subcommittee on Economic Stabilization of the Joint Committee on the Economic Report, *United States Monetary Policy: Recent Thinking and Experience: Hearings,* 83rd Congress, 2nd Session (Washington, D. C.: U. S. Government Printing Office, 1954), pp. 11-12.

[5] See Charles R. Whittlesey, "Reserve Requirements and the Integration of Credit Policies," *Quarterly Journal of Economics,* LVII (August 1944), 558-564.

ate and simultaneous impact of a given change in reserve requirements upon all member banks may be advantageous by comparison with the delayed influence of open-market operations upon member banks removed from the money-market center.[6]

Renewed suggestions that variable reserve ratios be adopted as an additional counter-inflationary weapon by the mother of central banks,[7] the Bank of England, contrast with the refusal of the American monetary authorities, already endowed with this tool for more than two decades, to apply it restrictively ever since early 1951. As shown in Table 1, all changes of member-bank reserve requirements in the United States since early 1951 to date have been in but one direction: downward. Thus, though unwilling to raise reserve requirements, the Federal Reserve has—presumably not to member bankers' discontent—shown willingness to lower reserve requirements. These diverse developments suggest that a reconsideration of reserve-requirement variation in comparison with open-market operations appears timely, both on theoretical and on policy grounds.

In line with the literature on the subject, the next three sections will assume a closed economy. In the final section this assumption will be dropped.

II. THE CASE OF RESTRICTION

Before analyzing the differential impact of open-market operations versus that of variation of reserve requirements, it is useful to specify the economic situation in which central-bank action is assumed to take place. Three types of situation may be distinguished.

[6] See Ira O. Scott, Jr., "The Regional Impact of Monetary Policy," *Quarterly Journal of Economics*, LXIX (May 1955), 283.

[7] See Sayers, *op. cit.*, p. 85, and his reference to Sir Theodore Gregory, *The Present Position of Central Bank*, 1955 Stamp Memorial Lecture (University of London: The Athlone Press, 1955), p. 21.

TABLE 1. *Member-bank Reserve Requirements in the United States, January 1951-June 1960*

(Per cent of deposits)

Effective date of change	Demand deposits			Time deposits	
	Central reserve. City banks	Reserve. City banks	Country banks	Central reserve and reserve. City banks	Country banks
1951: Jan. 11,16*	23	19	13	6	6
Jan. 25, Feb. 1*	24	20	14	. . . .	. . . .
1953: July 1, 9*	22	19	13	. . . .	. . . .
1954: June 16, 24*	21	. . . .	. . . .	5	5
July 29, Aug. 1*	20	18	12	. . . .	. . . .
1958: Feb. 27, Mar. 1*	19½	17½	11½	. . . .	. . . .
Mar. 20, Apr. 1*	19	17	11	. . . .	. . . .
Apr. 17	18½	. . . .	. . . .	. . . .	. . . .
Apr. 24	18	16½	. . . .	. . . .	. . . .
In effect June 1, 1960	18	16½	11	5	5

*First-of-month or mid-month dates are changes at country banks, and other dates are at central reserve city or reserve city banks.

Source: *Federal Reserve Bulletin*, XLVI (June 1960), 643.

In the first type of situation commercial banks are without significant excess reserves and are attempting to switch out of Government securities into private loans because of a boom in the demand for credit. This would be the state of affairs associated with a restrictive monetary policy.

In the second type of situation, too, commercial banks are without significant excess reserves but in equilibrium with respect to the structure of their assets. This would be the state of affairs associated with a "neutral" monetary policy.

In the third type of situation commercial banks have considerable or substantial excess reserves. This would be the state of affairs associated with an expansionary monetary policy. Let us take up these three types of situation in turn.

(i) Suppose that, being confronted with the first type of situation, the central bank has decided to reduce the volume of member-bank deposits by a given amount, and is considering whether to do so by open-market sale of Government securities or by raising member-bank reserve requirements. In this case, is it correct to say that there is no substantive difference between the effects of the two courses of action? Certainly not.

In the face of a boom in the demand for private credit the proximate objective of a restrictive monetary policy is to curb the switching by banks from Government securities into commercial loans. Yet the magnitude of such switching would be greater in response to newly raised reserve requirements than it would be in response to an equivalent sale of Government securities by the central bank. This outcome is due to two factors.

In the first place, the imposition of higher cash-reserve requirements reduces to zero the rate of return on a certain proportion of commercial banks' assets that have hitherto yielded a positive rate of return. In other words, the higher reserve requirements reduce not only the total volume of commercial-bank assets but also the proportion of commercial bank earning assets to their total assets. On the other hand, open-market operations reduce the total volume of commercial-bank assets without reducing the proportion of earnings assets to total assets. Thus, imposition of the higher reserve requirements has a more restrictive impact on commercial-bank income than the equivalent volume of open-market sales by the monetary authority. Therefore, the marginal utility of bank income is higher as a result of increased reserve requirements than as a result of open-market sales by the monetary authority.[8] The higher marginal utility of bank income induces commercial banks to

[8] Alternatively stated, the marginal rate of substitution of bank income for bank liquidity will be lower as a result of the rise in reserve requirements than as a result of open-market sales by the monetary authority. Cf. Earl R. Rolph, "Principles of Debt Management," *American Economic Review,* xlvii (June 1957), 319.

sacrifice liquidity, i.e., to shift further out of Government securities into loans, in order to obtain additional earnings.

Second, the liquidity needs of commercial banks are to a greater extent met by the reduced reserves themselves with a higher reserve requirement than with an unchanged reserve requirement.[9] To illustrate, if required reserves are 10 per cent, and bank deposits drop from 100 to 80, only 2 units of the 20 cash are available for paying off the deposits. On the other hand, if required reserves are 20 per cent, and deposits drop from 100 to 80, 4 units of the 20 cash are available for paying off the deposits. Thus the higher reserve requirements reduce the marginal utility of the "moneyness" of bank assets, also inducing commercial banks to sacrifice liquidity in order to obtain additional earnings.

Under conditions of a restrictive monetary policy, i.e., amid excess demand in the market for private credit, banks are afforded ample opportunity to offset the constraint placed upon them by the higher reserve requirements. The "income" effect and the "liquidity" effect of imposition of the requirements jointly induce banks to switch out of Government securities into loans on a larger scale than in response to open-market sales on the part of the monetary authority.

(ii) Our foregoing analysis of the first type of situation applies with but minor modification to the second type of situation. Here the "income" effect and the "liquidity" effect of an increase in reserve requirements will still take place. But since there is, by assumption, no excess demand for private credit, commercial-bank shifting from Government securities to loans will be smaller than in the first type of situation. In other words, the impact of imposition of higher reserve requirements will not be as perverse if, to begin with, commercial banks are in an equilibrium position with respect to the structure of their assets.

(iii) Though the third type of situation—widespread excess reserves in commercial banks—is commonly associated with an

[9] Cf. *Ibid.*

expansionary monetary policy, let us for the moment consider the implications of *higher* reserve requirements in this context. Here the imposition of higher reserve requirements produces neither the "income" effect nor the "liquidity" effect so long as the pre-existing excess cash reserves fully meet the higher reserve requirements. For as long as the higher reserve requirements can be satisfied without liquidation of earning assets, their imposition does not adversely affect the present income position of the banks involved; nor does it imply an increase in the proportion of liquid assets to total bank assets.

The upshot is that there exists an asymmetry between imposition of higher cash-reserve requirements and restrictive open-market operations by the central bank. Specifically, the following conclusions emerge:

(a) Amid a booming demand for credit, concomitant with a widespread absence of excess cash reserves in commercial banks, higher reserve requirements will induce more shifting by banks from Government securities to private loans than would restrictive open-market operations.

(b) In the absence of buoyant demand for credit and of excess reserves that could meet higher cash-reserve requirements, the higher requirements would still induce more shifting by banks from Government securities to loans than would restrictive open-market operations. This asymmetry, however, would not be as pronounced as under the conditions of conclusion (a).

(c) Amid widespread excess reserves that will fully satisfy higher cash-reserve requirements, the imposition of higher requirements constitutes no incentive for bank shifting from Government securities to private debt.

Manifestly, conclusions (a) and (b) must be qualified to the extent that there are differences in the reserve positions of different commercial banks. Likewise, conclusion (c) must be qualified to the extent that all or some banks lack excess cash reserves to fulfill the higher reserve requirements and are, therefore, compelled to liquidate earning assets.

III. IMPLICATIONS FOR THE RESTRICTION CONTROVERSY

We may now venture to re-assess the running controversy between various writers and the Federal Reserve on the comparative advantage of increases in reserve requirements versus restrictive open-market operations.

Our first and second conclusions rather severely circumscribe the validity of the argument that the shock effect of higher reserve requirements can be avoided by moderating the magnitude of the requirement increases. As implied by our third conclusion, this argument is applicable only to the type of situation wherein commercial banks possess sufficient excess reserves to meet higher reserve requirements without having to resort to the liquidation of earning assets.[10] And this kind of situation is rarely one that is associated with the choice between higher reserve requirements and restrictive open-market operations: rather, it is the kind of situation that is usually associated with the choice between lower reserve requirements and expansionary open-market operations. Thus, little support for the technique of increasing reserve requirements remains to be drawn even from our third conclusion: under the conditions which (apart from international transactions) give rise to consideration of the choice between higher reserve requirements and restrictive open-market operations, commercial banks are "loaned up" to begin with. Under such conditions, higher reserve requirements generate a shock effect upon commercial banks that is greater than the impact of restrictive open-market operations.

This difference in shock effect means that it is pointless to argue that more extensive use could be made of higher reserve

[10] This, indeed, is the type of situation adduced by Professor Sayers in his denial of an asymmetry between the two central-bank instruments. He uses for illustrative purposes the case in which, "with a normal cash reserve of 10 against deposits of 100 the banks hold excess reserves equal to 10," and compares the effect of an increase in the reserve ratio with that of restrictive open-market operations. Sayers, *op. cit.*, p. 89.

requirements if increases in requirements were made in very small fractions. Obviously, if a given increase in reserve requirements is minute, its shock effect is also likely to be minute. But this is hardly comforting. The point is that restrictive open-market operations generate less of a shock effect than correspondingly higher reserve requirements. Thus, if what is called for in a given case is *highly* restrictive central-bank action, the difference in the shock effects of the two instruments will be of much greater significance than if only *slightly* restrictive action is called for. In brief, substantial increases in reserve requirements will produce substantial differential shock effects; negligible increases in reserve requirements will produce negligible differential shock effects.

The differential shock effect of higher reserve requirements results from the fact that, in conditions wherein commercial banks are "loaned up" to begin with, higher reserve requirements are more deleterious to commercial-bank earnings than are restrictive open-market operations. Unawareness of this fact is at the bottom of the opposition to the Federal Reserve's views on the variation of reserve requirements.

Our conclusions also weaken the argument that changes in reserve requirements are preferable to open-market operations on the ground that the former will reduce time lags in the transmission of the effects of monetary policy to the commercial-banking system. If results of the variation of reserve requirements were the same as results of open-market operations in all respects but speed of transmission, preference for the former weapon over the latter would be quite plausible. We have seen, however, that there is an asymmetry in results, an asymmetry which militates against the increase of reserve requirements as a counter-inflationary measure. For one major objective of a restrictive monetary policy is to curb the expansion of commercial-bank credit to private borrowers. This objective is thwarted by the variation of reserve requirements in comparison with the use of open-market operations. When, in addition, differences between the two weapons in administrative flexibility and in ease of reversibility are taken into account, little is left of the case for the use of increases in reserve requirements as a short-period alternative to restrictive open-market operations.

IV. THE CASE OF EXPANSION

Like other techniques of monetary control, the variation of cash-reserve requirements is a double-edged sword: requirements can be lowered, as well as increased. Thus far we have considered only the case of an increase in requirements versus restrictive open-market operations. As previously mentioned, however, the situation of widespread excess reserves is commonly the setting for an expansionary monetary policy, i.e., for choice by the central bank between lowering cash-reserve requirements and performing open-market purchases. Hence, we now turn to the case of expansionary measures.

A reduction of reserve requirements augments immediately and simultaneously the lending capacity of all member banks. In contrast, the central bank's purchase of Government securities affects, in the first instance, the lending capacity of only those institutions that are sellers of the securities purchased by the central bank. It appears, therefore, that when faced with a downturn in economic activity, the central bank should prefer the reduction of reserve requirements to the purchase of Government securities. As monetary policy is generally deemed to be more potent in curbing inflation than in reversing recession, resort to the more spectacular measure of cutting reserve requirements seems particularly inviting.

In this vein, the Chairman of the Federal Reserve Board has stated,

> So far as I am aware, no one has questioned the effectiveness of reserve requirement reductions, or the fact that they have an important advantage over the other general instru-

ments in a recession. Decreased reserve requirements affect all banks immediately and place every bank in the country under simultaneous pressure to lend or invest in order to maximize its earnings, whereas open-market purchases have less immediate impact on many country banks.[11]

Thus, in the view of the Federal Reserve, rapidity of impression upon member banks imparts a comparative advantage to the reduction of reserve requirements over open-market purchases. Is, however, rapidity of impression upon member banks so decisive a point in favor of reduction of reserve requirements? Are there no equally weighty, or even weightier, drawbacks to the reduction of reserve requirements as compared with open-market purchases?

Consider the matter of generating pressure that will induce member banks to lend or invest in order to maximize their earnings. By augmenting their lending capacity, a reduction in reserve requirements merely makes it possible for member banks to increase their loans and investments. On the other hand, open-market purchases by the central bank reduce the volume of income-producing Government securities in the portfolios of their sellers and, therefore, in the hands of the private economy generally. In other words, a reduction of reserve requirements immediately enables all member banks to increase their earning assets, while the central bank's open-market purchase immediately decreases the earning assets of those that have liquidated Government securities.

So far, then, as the member banks that have sold Government securities in the open market are concerned, their immediate incentive to lend or invest is greater under the impact of the central bank's open-market purchase than under the impact of reduced reserve requirements. For a reduction in reserve require-

---

[11] Answer by the Chairman of the Board of Governors of the Federal Reserve System in United States Congress, Joint Economic Committee, *Employment, Growth, and Price Levels: Hearings,* Part 6A, 86th Congress, 1st Session (Washington, D. C.: U. S. Government Printing Office, 1959), p. 1497.

ments would not have diminished their earning assets, while their open-market liquidation of Government securities has actually diminished their earning assets. Hence, the marginal utility of income for participating member banks is higher under the impact of expansionary open-market operations than under the impact of reduced reserve requirements. Alternatively stated, the incentive to replenish a diminished volume of earning assets is greater than the incentive to augment an undiminished volume of earning assets.

But what of the member banks, particularly country banks, that would not participate in the central bank's expansionary open-market activity? It is plausible that the country banks most prone to abstain from such open-market activity are also prone to be slowest in activating excess cash reserves generated by a reduction of reserve requirements. Moreover, in contrast to the nonparticipating member banks, there are financial institutions other than commercial banks that do participate in open-market activity: the market for Government securities extends far beyond the central and commercial banks. And like the member banks that would participate in a given open-market activity, the other participating financial institutions would also have greater immediate incentive to lend or invest under the impact of the central bank's open-market purchase than under the impact of a reduction in reserve requirements, which would not apply to them in any event.

Furthermore, the Federal Reserve's above-quoted comparison of open-market operations with reserve requirement variation presupposes a highly limiting interpretation of open-market operations, namely: operations confined to the short-term sector of the Government securities market. (This presupposition derives from the Federal Reserve's "bills-only" policy to be examined in Chapter 4.) It so happens that such a limiting interpretation places open-market operations in the weakest possible position by comparison with the reduction of cash-reserve requirements. For confinement of open-market operations to the short-term sector means renunciation of direct central-bank influence upon interest rates and credit availability in maturity sectors other than the short-term sector. On the other hand, if we adopt an interpretation of open-market operations whereby such operations are not confined to a particular maturity sector to the exclusion of other sectors, the usefulness of open-market operations can be assessed in full measure.

We, therefore, adopt the more general interpretation of open-market operations. The contrast between reduction of cash-reserve requirements and expansionary open-market operations now stands out clearly. A reduction of cash-reserve requirements merely makes it possible for all member banks to expand their lending activity as they see fit. Expansionary open-market operations, however, constitute direct central-bank easing action that can be aimed at one or more maturity sectors as the central bank sees fit. Thus, while reduction of cash-reserve requirements places the central bank at the mercy of commercial banks so far as the timing, extent, and distribution of easing action are concerned, open-market operations enable the central bank to take the easing action directly, immediately, and flexibly. As the swiftness, size, and maturity-sector of credit-easing action may be crucial in maximizing the contribution of monetary policy to the stemming or reversing of a business downturn, the comparative advantage of open-market operations is decisive.

To summarize, there is an asymmetry between reduction of cash-reserve requirements and expansionary open-market operations. The asymmetry militates against the former instrument and in favor of the latter in two respects. First, due to the differential impact of the two techniques upon the volume of earning assets of commercial banks and others, expansionary open-market operations exert greater pressure on these institutions to lend or invest than does reduction of reserve requirements. Second, expansionary open-market operations do, while reduction of reserve requirements does not, enable the central bank to determine directly the rapidity, the extent, and the maturity sector of its credit-easing action upon the credit market.

V . QUALIFICATION

Would it be warranted to conclude that adoption of the reserve-variation weapon is entirely without merit? Not quite.

In economies where a Government securities market is lacking or where the central bank's portfolio of Government securities is too meager for the use of open-market operations, the additional instrument of changing reserve requirements is well nigh indispensable. Yet, as the Government securities market in such economies expands over time—due, say, to a growing national debt in the course of Governmental deficit financing of economic-development projects—open-market operations may become an increasingly practicable alternative to variation of reserve requirements.

Even in economies with a considerable Government securities market and with a central bank in possession of a moderately sizable securities portfolio, there is reason to endow the central bank with both instruments. Suppose that an economy is experiencing, as was the United States in the mid-1930s, a heavy inflow of gold and that the central bank seeks to neutralize the potentially expansionary effect of this inflow upon the domestic money supply. To absorb the commercial banks' excess cash reserves by means of open-market operations could come near to wiping out the central bank's portfolio of Government securities. On the other hand, to absorb the increase in excess reserves by means of higher cash-reserve requirements for commercial banks would keep intact the central bank's stock of Government securities for continued use of domestic monetary policy. Thus, the variation of cash-reserve requirements is not devoid of all merit as a technique of monetary control, particularly in a world of open economies.

3

SUPPLEMENTARY

SECURITY-RESERVE

REQUIREMENTS

I. THE PROPOSAL

In most Western economies, initial reaction to the massive
growth of Government debt during and following World War II
was one of caution about newly intensified problems rather than
one of eagerness to seize newly developed opportunities. The
problems immediately and generally recognized were those of
debt management; the opportunities only later and less fully
acknowledged were those of monetary control.

In the postwar American economy, as well as elsewhere, the
intricate task of managing a large and widely dispersed national
debt has placed in question the appropriateness of flexible interest-rate policies, i.e., the uninhibited use of open-market operations as an instrument of central banking. Particularly since
the restoration of American central banking to an active role as
a result of the Treasury-Federal Reserve Accord of March 1951,
the view has been expressed that it would be both feasible and
desirable to shield Government securities, in whole or in part,
from the effects of counter-inflationary monetary policy upon

the private credit market.[1] One proposal frequently made in this connection is to require Government securities as part of the reserve to be held by commercial banks against their deposit liabilities, supplementary to the prevailing cash-reserve requirements. As an alternative to holding required securities, commercial banks would be permitted to hold cash.

In recent years, supplementary security-reserve requirements have been enforced in various countries. In the United States, the suggestion of such requirements was made at the outbreak of World War II, repeated toward the end of the war and shortly thereafter, discussed at length in subsequent Congressional hearings, particularly in replies to the 1952 Patman Committee, and revived in still more recent critiques of restrictive Federal Reserve policy.[2]

Yet, as early as 1946, one analysis of supplementary requirements included a hypothesis which—if it had been noted and

[1] See replies by economists in United States Congress, Joint Committee on the Economic Report, *Monetary Policy and Management of the Public Debt: Replies to Questions and Other Material for Use of the Subcommittee on General Credit Control and Debt Management* (Patman Committee), 82nd Congress, 2nd Session (Washington, D. C.: U. S. Government Printing Office, 1952), pp. 1081-1092. Most of the responding economists did not deem the insulation of Government securities from the impact of restrictive monetary policy desirable; but many of these economists considered such insulation possible at least in part. About a third of the responding economists believed that insulation of a considerable part of the national debt would be both possible and desirable. At least two, Seymour E. Harris and Louis Shere, stated that it would be both possible and desirable to insulate all public-debt securities.

See also *ibid.*, pp. 1299-1300, Statement by Conference of University Economists, recommending "serious examination with a view to possible adoption" of several devices for moderating the impact of restrictive monetary policy on the prices and yields of Government securities. Milton Friedman and Charles J. Hitch dissented from this recommendation.

[2] See Lawrence H. Seltzer, "The Problem of Our Excessive Banking Reserves," *Journal of the American Statistical Association*, xxxv (March 1940), pp. 32-36; Seltzer, "The Changed Environment of Monetary-Banking Policy," *American Economic Review*, xxxvi (May 1946), 76-79; "Pro-

confirmed by other writers—could have dispelled much of the subsequent support for such requirements. As stated by its authors without further elaboration, one "fundamental principle" of a system of security reserves is that "reserve requirements be revised sufficiently to absorb the bulk of the governments which banks hold."[3] It seems somewhat surprising that few contemporary proponents of supplementary requirements in the United States have accorded explicit attention to this "fundamental principle." For if valid, this principle would imply (a) either widely different supplementary requirements for different banks or else a wholesale reshaping of the asset structure of numerous banks, *and* (b) virtual exclusion of banks from participation in open-market activity for the duration of the supplementary requirements.

Such far-reaching implications call for detailed reconsideration of the case for supplementary security-reserve requirements. We devote the present chapter to this reconsideration within the setting of the American monetary system and in light of propositions that were applied in Chapter II to the comparison between open-market operations versus reserve-requirement variation.

posal for a Special Reserve Requirement against the Demand and Time Deposits of Banks," *Federal Reserve Bulletin,* xxxiv (January 1948), 14-23 (a proposal submitted to the Committee on Banking and Currency of the United States House of Representatives in December 1947); Patman Committee, *op. cit.,* pp. 121-129, 477-489; Emanuel A. Goldenweiser, *American Monetary Policy* (New York: McGraw-Hill Book Company, 1951), pp. 61-63; Albert G. Hart, *Defense and the Dollar* (New York: Twentieth Century Fund, 1953), pp. 42-45, 86-89; Ervin Miller, "Monetary Policy in a Changing World," *Quarterly Journal of Economics,* lxx (February 1956), 27-28, 38-43; Warren L. Smith, "On the Effectiveness of Monetary Policy," *American Economic Review,* xlvi (September 1956), 606; and additional references below.

3 Melvin G. de Chazeau, Albert G. Hart, *et al., Jobs and Markets* (New York: McGraw-Hill Book Company, 1946), p. 93. Hart restated this principle in Max Millikan (editor), *Income Stabilization for a Developing Democracy* (New Haven: Yale University Press, 1953), p. 322.

II. OBJECTIVES

Prerequisite to the analysis of supplementary security-reserve requirements is recognition of the different objectives they are intended to serve. Supplementary requirements may be directed at any of several objectives.

One objective may be to assure the solvency of commercial banks by compelling them to hold some low-risk assets.[4] Thus, supplementary security-reserve requirements may be sought as a device for minimizing bank failures.

A second objective may arise where the central bank is committed to peg interest rates on Government securities and thus to permit monetization of Government debt. In order to reduce the inflationary potential of bank holdings of Government securities without increasing *cash*-reserve requirements, supplementary security reserve requirements may be instituted. Here the supplementary requirements have the dual purpose of (1) reducing (or stopping) bank movement out of Government securities into private debt, and (2) simultaneously allowing a higher level of bank earnings than under increased cash-reserve requirements.[5]

[4] See Edward C. Simmons, "Secondary Reserve Requirements for Banks," *American Economic Review*, XLI (March 1951), 135: "The adoption of a secondary reserve requirement would operate in the same direction as the old [commercial-loan] theory in that it would lead banks to hold low risk assets. A large portion of bank assets would not be affected, but a substantial gain would result from requiring banks to confine a large portion of their resources to low risk categories. Past experience with wholesale bank failures justifies obliging bank management to limit the choice of assets by means of a secondary reserve requirement."

[5] The above-cited proposal by the Federal Reserve Board illustrates this point. In commenting on it, the Board noted: "It has been suggested that the same result [as that to be attained by the special reserve measure] might be achieved by an increase in existing basic reserve requirements of banks. If this were done, however, banks would have to meet the increase by selling Government securities, which the Federal Reserve System would have to buy in order to supply the needed reserves. This would decrease the banks' earning assets and their earnings, whereas the proposed special reserve measure would enable them to retain earning assets. The continued profitability of bank operations is essential if the banks are to meet their

A third objective may be to hold down the cost of servicing the national debt without committing the central bank to peg interest rates on Government securities. The following situations are here separable. (a) In an underdeveloped economy, supplementary requirements may be sought as a means of creating or supporting a market for Government securities and thereby fostering the deficit financing of the Government's economic-development activities.[6] (b) In a wartime economy, supplementary requirements may be favored as a measure of war finance.[7] (c) In an advanced peacetime economy, supplementary requirements may be advocated as a device for insulating Government securities, in whole or in part, from the impact of restrictive monetary policy on the private credit market.[8]

costs and build up adequate reserves while serving their communities constructively." "Proposal for a Special Reserve Requirement against Demand and Time Deposits of Banks," pp. 18-19. See also Lawrence H. Seltzer, "Control of Bank Portfolios as an Instrument of Monetary Control," *American Economic Review*, XLII (May 1952), 241-242.

[6] Contemporary security-reserve requirements in certain Asian and Latin American countries illustrate this point. See Patman Committee, *op. cit.*, pp. 172-173, 194, 516. The justification for the requirements is presumably the view that Government deficits are more productive or more conducive to economic development than would be private uses of the loanable funds involved.

[7] National security-reserve requirements adopted in the United States during the Civil War are an illustration. It has been stated that in subsequent years these requirements fostered the development of a market for United States Government obligations. Davis R. Dewey, *Financial History of the United States*, 10th Edition (New York: Longmans, Green and Company, 1928), pp. 325-328; and Chester W. Wright, *Economic History of the United States*, 2nd Edition (New York: McGraw-Hill Book Company, 1948), pp. 178-179. It has, however, also been suggested that American security-reserve requirements became a major factor in the inflexibility of national bank currency to the "needs" of business and commercial agriculture in the thirty-five years following the Civil War. Paul Studenski and Herman E. Krooss, *Financial History of the United States* (New York: McGraw-Hill Book Company, 1952), pp. 178-179.

[8] Nearly all proposals of security-reserve requirements made in the United States since the Treasury-Federal Reserve Accord of 1951 apply to this situation. For a sketch of security-reserve requirements in contemporary

Cognizance of the diversity of objectives and situations outlined above indicates that there is no inherent inconsistency between favoring security-reserve requirements in a setting relevant to one objective and opposing such requirements in a setting relevant to a different objective. It may be pointed out, for example, that compulsory holding of United States Government bonds was instituted (and retained for many years later) under the National Banking Act during the Civil War, that the Federal Reserve Board advocated a security-reserve plan in the immediate postwar situation of pegged bond prices, that laws regulating the operation of state banks in some parts of the United States include security-reserve requirements, and that other countries have, as previously noted, instituted such requirements in recent years. From none of these observations, however, does it necessarily follow that the central bank in the present-day American setting should be more favorably inclined than it now is to follow suit and impose security-reserve requirements. "Historical perspective," which has been called for in a recent plea for their adoption in the United States, certainly suggests that the newness of security-reserve requirements is "more apparent than real."[9] But historical perspective also suggests that it may be quite misleading to infer from the existence of such requirements in one setting their desirability in an essentially different setting.

This chapter is confined to supplementary security-reserve requirements with the objective of insulating bank-held Government debt, in whole or in part, from the impact of restrictive monetary policy on the private-credit market. Assuming that the reserve-eligible securities are either nonmarketable or else of

West European economies, see Sir Frederick W. Leith-Ross, *Orthodox Credit Control in Post-War Conditions* (Rotterdam: Institut International d'Etudes Bancaires, 1957), pp. 39 ff.; for a more comprehensive survey, see Peter G. Fousek, *Foreign Central Banking: The Instruments of Monetary Policy* (New York: Federal Reserve Bank of New York, 1957), pp. 57-68.

[9] Miller, *op. cit.*, p. 41.

specially designated and limited marketable issues, the supplementary requirements have two facets. First, they enable the Treasury to hold down interest rates on the securities that banks are compelled to hold. Second, the requirements enable the central bank to prevent switching by member banks from the immobilized securities into other earning assets. Thus, as an insulation technique, supplementary requirements are both a tool of debt management and an instrument of credit control.

Dominant in the contemporary American setting for the insulation objective is a maturity distribution of Government debt that entails relatively frequent and sizable refinancing operations by the Treasury. Pertaining to the end of 1959, Table 2 illustrates the maturity distribution of marketable United States Government debt. Thus, in December 1959 about 42 per cent of total marketable Government securities and 22 per cent of marketable Government securities held by commercial banks were within one year of maturity. With such a maturity distribution, the prospect of higher interest rates is of substantial consequence for the total cost of servicing Government debt. The quest for new devices to hold down the interest burden of the Treasury may, therefore, be expected to continue for years to come.

TABLE 2. *Maturity Classification of U. S. Government Marketable Securities, December 31, 1959*

		(Par value in millions of dollars)			
Type of holder	Total	Within 1 year	1-5 years	5-10 years	Over 10 years
All holders	188,269	78,456	61,609	23,625	24,579
Commercial banks	51,841	11,198	28,778	9,235	2,629

Source: *Federal Reserve Bulletin*, XLVI (May 1960), 535.

One difficulty likely to face any attempt at instituting and maintaining supplementary security-reserve requirements in the present setting will not be treated here. This is the matter of extending the applicability of the security requirements to other financial institutions (such as savings banks, savings and loan associations, and life insurance companies). We set this matter aside not because it may safely be regarded as negligible by comparison with the problems to be examined. On the contrary, if the security-reserve requirements were not extended to all financial institutions, those not subject to the requirements would be placed at a distinct competitive advantage in that they would remain free to switch at will out of Government securities into private debt.[10] Moreover, to the extent that the supply of Government securities to the open market by those subject to the requirements were curtailed, the exempt institutions would be induced to shift out of Government securities on a larger scale

[10] It might seem that an analogous argument could also be used against the imposition and increase of cash-reserve requirements that are confined to commercial banks. But the analogy is incorrect: the singling out of commercial banks for a cash-reserve requirement is, as expounded in Chapter 8, founded upon the fact that, among private financial institutions, only commercial banks have the capacity to engage in the creation of money. Therefore, control over the creation of money is the ground for imposing upon commercial banks a cash-reserve requirement and for varying it at the discretion of the monetary authority. On the other hand, in regard to switching from Government securities into private debt, commercial banks are on the same footing with all other financial institutions. Hence, to single out commercial banks for a security-reserve requirement is a fundamentally different proposition from the one to single them out for a cash-reserve requirement.

A correct analogy to our argument against the singling out of commercial banks for a security-reserve requirement is the argument that a cash-reserve requirement for member commercial banks places nonmember commercial banks at a competitive advantage, insofar as the cash-reserve requirement imposed by the Federal Reserve exceeds the requirement imposed by states. Fortunately, more than 80 per cent of total demand deposits in the United States are at member banks. Nonetheless, it remains true that the rationale for imposing a cash-reserve requirement upon member commercial banks is equally applicable to nonmember commercial banks. Hence, the logical implication of the competitive advantage enjoyed by nonmember commercial banks is not that the cash-reserve requirement imposed by the Federal Reserve ought to be abolished, but rather that all commercial banks ought to be subjected to that requirement.

than otherwise. Nevertheless, it appears instructive to explore the use of supplementary security-reserve requirements limited to member banks even in abstraction from this added difficulty.

III. TIMING OF IMPOSITION

In the discussion of supplementary security-reserve requirements with the insulation objective, it is generally taken for granted that the requirements would be imposed and possibly raised as part of a restrictive monetary policy. In other words, it is implicitly supposed that the imposition and possible increase of the requirements would be so timed as to take place when there existed excess demand in the market for private credit. While this is an entirely plausible assumption, it should be noted that requirements imposed in a period of an expansionary or "neutral" monetary policy could also be designed to provide at least partial insulation of bank-held Government debt for subsequent periods of inflation. Accordingly, let us first consider the case of the imposition of requirements during a period of sizable inflationary pressures and later turn to alternative cases.

With reference to a given excess demand in the market for private credit, two components of a bank's holdings of Government securities may be distinguished.[11] That part of its holdings which (in the absence of supplementary requirements) a bank would unload in the open market and/or run off in seeking to shift into other earning assets, may be termed its "extra-marginal"

---

[11] In determining its asset structure, a commercial bank must constantly weigh its earnings position versus its liquidity position. At any one time, the average rate of return on Government securities is likely to be lower than the average rate of return on other earning assets. With a widening of the earnings differential due to excess demand in the private credit market, banks will tend to move out of Government securities into other earning assets up to the point where the disadvantage of a further reduction of liquidity is deemed to offset the advantage of a further rise in earnings.

holdings. Correspondingly, that part of its holdings which (in the absence of supplementary requirements) the bank would retain, may be termed its "intra-marginal" holdings.

Supplementary security-reserve requirements that merely immobilized intra-marginal holdings would still necessitate open-market operations at the active margins where banks attempt to shift from Government securities to other earning assets.[12] Furthermore, with some securities newly immobilized by supplementary requirements, the banks' incentive to shift out of remaining Government securities would be increased for two reasons.

In the first place, the newly imposed requirements are presumably designed to prevent interest rates on required reserve securities from rising: it is in this sense that the securities absorbed by the requirements are "insulated" from the impact of restrictive monetary policies. Thus, imposition of the supplementary requirements limits the rate of return on a certain proportion of banks' earning assets to a lower level than in the absence of the requirements, implying a smaller bank income than otherwise. This increases the marginal utility of bank income, inducing banks to sacrifice liquidity to obtain additional earnings.

Second, the needs of banks for liquid assets will to a greater extent be met by the reserves themselves with a higher total reserve requirement (primary plus supplementary combined) than with a lower one. This reduces the marginal utility of the "moneyness" of bank assets, also inducing banks to sacrifice liquidity to obtain additional earnings.

Under conditions of a restrictive monetary policy, i.e., amid excess demand in the market for private credit, banks are afforded ample opportunity to offset the constraint placed upon them by supplementary requirements that lock in only some portion of their intra-marginal holdings. The "income" effect

12 Robert V. Roosa, "Integrating Debt Management and Open Market Operations," *American Economic Review*, XLII (May 1952), 223.

and the "liquidity" effect of the imposition of the requirements jointly induce banks to switch out of freely disposable Government securities into loans on a larger scale than they would have in the absence of the newly imposed requirements. Thus, from the viewpoint of credit control, the imposition of requirements that immobilize only a part of banks' intra-marginal holdings will have a perverse impact: switching by banks from Government securities to loans will be stimulated rather than curtailed. And attempts by the monetary authorities to prevent the volume of bank loans from rising are likely to involve greater, rather than smaller, open-market operations than in the absence of the newly imposed requirements.

Nor does it, under such circumstances, necessarily follow that imposition of the supplementary requirements will produce the intended result from the viewpoint of the interest burden of the Treasury. To be sure, yields on required reserve securities could be held constant or could even be reduced by decree. But, with increased unloading by banks of freely disposable Government securities, successful refinancing of these securities would necessitate their carrying higher interest rates than otherwise. The precise net effect of imposition of the supplementary requirements on the Treasury's interest burden would differ with the height of the requirements, the types of Government securities they absorb, the rates of return on reserve securities, and the size, composition, and yields of freely disposable Government securities conducive to successful refinancing by the Treasury.

On the other hand, if the supplementary requirements absorb their entire intra-marginal holdings, banks will be unable to unload and/or run off more Government securities than they would have anyway. In this instance, it necessarily follows that the requirements will have the desired effect on the interest burden of the Treasury: yields on absorbed securities can be kept constant, while banks are prevented from reducing their holdings any more than they would have in any event.

The years 1955 and 1956 may serve as illustrations of the approximate magnitude of extra-marginal holdings. Between December 31, 1954, and December 31, 1955, member banks reduced their holdings of Government securities by 12.3 per cent; between the latter date and December 31, 1956, the reduction was by 6.1 per cent.[13] The year 1955 was characterized by recovery from a mild recession rather than by conditions associated with a restrictive monetary policy; thus, the figure of 12.3 per cent is probably an overstatement of extra-marginal holdings in a period of tight money. But even if intra-marginal holdings account for no more than 90 per cent of aggregate member-bank holdings of Government securities, it seems appropriate to regard them as constituting the "bulk" of such holdings.

Let us now turn to the less likely case of imposition of the supplementary requirements at a time of expansionary monetary policy. In this instance, the requirements need not absorb the bulk of bank-held Government debt in order to be effective from the viewpoint of either credit policy or debt management. The inducement for banks to switch from freely disposable Government securities to loans will be drastically limited by the implied deficiency of demand in the private credit market. To the extent that banks do engage in such switching, the central bank will readily encourage it by means of open-market purchases: such purchases harmonize with an expansionary policy. Such purchases also imply smaller Treasury interest payments to the private sector than otherwise.

Finally, we may take up the case of "neutral" monetary policy: high-level employment without strong inflationary pressures. Here, in response to newly imposed supplementary requirements that do not absorb the bulk of bank-held Government debt, the incentive for banks to shift from freely disposable Government securities to loans is presumably limited by the absence of significant excess demand in the private credit market. The

[13] Computed from *Federal Reserve Bulletin*, XLIII (October 1957), 1149.

precise magnitude of such shifting will depend on the rates of return on reserve securities as compared to rates on Government securities prior to the imposition of the requirements.

In sum, unless they absorb the bulk of bank-held Government debt, supplementary security-reserve requirements imposed in a period of restrictive monetary policy will produce a perverse impact from the viewpoint of credit control and will not necessarily serve their desired objective from the viewpoint of debt management. These adverse consequences may be avoided (or reduced) by imposition of the requirements in a period of expansionary (or "neutral") monetary policy.

IV. STRUCTURE

In assessing the feasibility of supplementary security-reserve requirements directed at the insulation objective, it is necessary to consider not only the timing aspect but also the structural aspect of such requirements, i.e., the method of determining the height of required supplementary reserve ratios for different banks. Assuming that there exist significant differences in the relative size and composition of different banks' holdings of Government securities, it must be decided whether (a) the supplementary reserve ratios should be uniform and sufficiently low to permit swift compliance with the requirements by the great majority of banks; (b) the height of the ratios should be different for different banks, depending on relative size and composition of their holdings of Government securities; (c) the height of the ratio should be uniform and determined without regard to differences in holdings of the separate banks; or (d) some compromise of the preceding approaches should be adopted. Approach (a) will seriously limit the usefulness of the requirements; (b) will necessitate significantly different supplementary reserve ratios for different banks—a move in the opposite direction from that of contemporary thinking and suggestions with regard to member-bank cash-reserve requirements;[14] (c) will entail wholesale changes in the structure of earning assets of different banks; and (d) may so complicate the structure of reserve requirements as to render the whole scheme unfeasible and inferior to direct regulation of member-bank lending activity. Thus, much depends on the extent of diversity in the different banks' holdings of Government securities.

A recent breakdown of member banks by classes indicates that the ratio of Government securities to total assets varied from 19.1 per cent for central reserve city banks in New York to 32.8 per cent for all country banks.[15] Lest one hasten to conclude that supplementary security-reserve requirements could conveniently be patterned after the present structure of cash-reserve requirements, the following additional data should be noted.

A recent geographical breakdown of all member banks shows that the ratio of Government securities to total assets ranged from 21.8 per cent for member banks in the New York Federal Reserve district to 33.9 per cent for the Chicago district.[16] A geographical breakdown of all Reserve city member banks indicates a range of the same ratio from 16.0 per cent in the Philadelphia district to 35.0 per cent in the Chicago district.[17]

A breakdown of all insured commercial banks by size group shows that, whereas certificates of indebtedness constituted 13.1 per cent of total holdings of Government securities in banks of smallest size, that ratio was 5.8 per cent in banks of next to the largest size.[18] While the ratio of marketable bonds maturing

[14] For a review of such thinking and suggestions see Federal Reserve Bank of New York, *Bank Reserves* (New York: 1951), pp. 5-10; and Economic Policy Commission, American Bankers Association, *Member Bank Reserve Requirements* (New York: 1957), pp. 74-98.

[15] *Federal Reserve Bulletin*, XLIII (June 1957), 715.

[16] *Ibid.*, p. 716.

[17] *Ibid.*, p. 717.

[18] Federal Deposit Insurance Corporation, *Annual Report for the Year Ended December 31, 1954* (Washington, D. C.: 1955), p. 72.

after five years to total holdings of Government securities was 21.5 per cent in banks of the smallest size, it was 44.7 per cent in banks of the largest size.[19]

With regard to the imposition and possible increase in supplementary security-reserve requirements as part of an anti-inflationary monetary policy, the foregoing statistical illustrations are quite suggestive. Supplementary security-reserve requirements sufficiently high to absorb the bulk of Government securities in the possession of banks in one section of the country may prove grossly inadequate for other sections. Alternatively, requirements that will immobilize the bulk of Government securities held by banks in one region may be excessively high for other regions. In the former instance, sizable intra-marginal holdings may be left freely disposable in certain areas. In the latter instance, banks in some regions may have to liquidate private loans and investments in large proportions, with resulting credit stringency and substantial changes in the role of such banks in the communities they serve.

If the height of the supplementary requirements were made to reflect regional differences in the relative importance of Government security holdings, it would be found that this course would not overcome the uneven distribution of Government securities in other important respects. As previously noted, marketable bonds maturing in more than five years were of substantially greater importance for banks of large size than for those of small. In order to avert large-scale run-offs of shorter-term securities, which were relatively more important in small-sized banks, it would seem appropriate to gear reserve requirements to size group as well as to regional location. But this would lead to requirements that would absorb a higher proportion of the smaller banks' holdings than of the larger. An interesting by-product of this approach would be a greater reduction in the latitude of choice and in the earnings potential of smaller banks than in those of larger banks. It appears doubtful that either the Federal

19 *Ibid.*

Reserve or the Treasury would deliberately seek to enforce a structure of reserve requirements to the clear disadvantage of smaller banks.

One possible way out of this dilemma may be to set the supplementary requirements with reference to the magnitude and composition of holdings on a given date or over a given period in the recent past. This course, however, will lead to widely different supplementary requirements for different banks. Once so drastic a departure from commonly accepted notions of a proper structure of reserve requirements is advocated in the name of credit control, the logical conclusion would be to regulate the volume of member-bank lending directly,[20] rather than indirectly, by means of centralized control of the volume of banks' holdings of Government securities. The direct approach would avoid the perverse impact of supplementary requirements that immobilized only a part of intra-marginal holdings; in addition, it would prevent possible switching into loans from state and local government securities as well as from United States Government obligations.

V. DESIRABILITY

It is widely acknowledged that, with respect to flexibility in adjustment to changing circumstances, monetary policy is superior to fiscal policy.[21] This superiority is of particular importance in counteracting inflationary pressures, because it is primarily as an anti-inflationary force that the potency of monetary policy has been recognized. Yet, as brought out in the preceding

[20] For a suggested scheme see Martin Bronfenbrenner, "A Loan Ratio for Inflation Control," *Journal of Political Economy*, LIX (October 1951), 420-433.

[21] See, for example, Smith, *op. cit.*, p. 605; James G. Maxwell, *Fiscal Policy* (New York: Henry Holt and Company, 1955), pp. 19-22; Kenyon E. Poole, *Public Finance and Economic Welfare* (New York: Rinehart and Company, 1956), pp. 430-433.

chapter, different tools of central banking do not contribute equally to the adaptability of monetary policy to contra-cyclical change. Particularly suggestive in connection with supplementary security-reserve requirements is experience with variation of cash-reserve requirements. As reported by the Federal Reserve,

> . . . experience with the reserve requirement instrument up to the present time has shown it to be inherently less flexible than the discount and open market instruments, at least under conditions where restraint on credit expansion is desirable, and therefore this instrument has tended to be used less to meet short-run changes in credit conditions and more to make adjustments to unusual and large changes in bank reserve positions brought about by special conditions. This inflexibility has resulted principally from the fact that a change in reserve requirements immediately and directly affects every member bank, or at least every member bank in one or more of the three reserve classifications (central reserve city, reserve city and country banks). No account can be taken of the situation of individual banks, no matter how much they may merit exceptions. To avoid unnecessary hardships so far as possible, exhaustive studies or time-consuming tests have usually been made before increasing reserve requirements. The delay itself has tended to weaken the effectiveness of the action eventually taken.[22]

The proposal that security-reserve requirements should be varied with about the same frequency as the Federal Reserve Banks' discount rate[23] could hardly seem plausible to a monetary authority not seeking to reduce its own adaptability to changing conditions. To the studies, investigations, tests, deliberations, considerations of equity and of relative competitive position that would surround every change in security-reserve requirements must be added the prospect of perverse impact of increases in the requirements in periods of restrictive monetary policy. The case against short-term variation of supplementary requirements is indeed overwhelming.

[22] Patman Committee, *op. cit.*, pp. 465-466.
[23] Miller, *op. cit.*, p. 40.

There remains, however, the question whether it would not be desirable to institute supplementary security-reserve requirements that would be subject only to infrequent variation. Such requirements could permanently, or for relatively long periods, immunize the securities they absorbed from open-market influences. Thus, such requirements would be rather similar to higher cash-reserve requirements, the one significant difference being that security reserves would yield their holder a positive rate of return, whereas cash reserves presumably would not. This point of difference implies that, in terms of the burden of servicing Government debt, the imposition of higher cash-reserve requirements is preferable to the imposition of supplementary security-reserve requirements; for interest on reserve securities would be paid by the Government to private institutions and would, therefore, affect the economy's tax burden. On the other hand, interest on securities acquired by the Federal Reserve (in accommodating the high cash requirements of banks) would largely revert to the Treasury without affecting the economy's tax burden.[24]

The possibility of higher cash-reserve requirements as an alternative to security-reserve requirements assumes special significance, once a fundamental issue that underlies the insulation objective is made explicit. The issue is whether the monetary authorities should be equipped with an instrument whose application would, in effect, constitute a deviation from the principle on which the existing separation of Treasury from central bank rests. According to this principle, the Treasury should not be permitted to borrow funds on terms to be subject to its dictation alone. Instead, the Treasury should generally be faced with the

[24] Approximately 90 per cent of the Federal Reserve Banks' annual net earnings after payment of dividends to member banks are now being paid over to the Treasury. In 1956, for example, Federal Reserve Banks' net earnings after payment of dividends were $455.5 million. Of this amount, $401.5 million (or 88 per cent) was paid over to the Treasury (under the label "interest on Federal Reserve notes"). *Federal Reserve Bulletin*, XLIV (February 1957), 210.

necessity to bid for funds outside the central bank in competition with other borrowers. Consequently, yields on Government securities are not to be disconnected from the market mechanism that sets interest rates. Insofar as the suggestion of supplementary security-reserve requirements seeks to break the connection between yields on national debt and the credit-market mechanism, it abandons the principle on which the existing separation of Treasury from central bank is founded.

In defense of this principle, it has been suggested that consolidation of the fiscal and central banking powers in the Treasury may lead to excessive reliance on creation of money and to the avoidance of appropriate fiscal policies when these consist of increased taxation or reduced government expenditures or both.[25] There are, of course, cogent arguments against the principle underlying the separation of Treasury from central bank, but their acceptance would do little to strengthen the case for supplementary security-reserve requirements. For, once it is granted that the Treasury should generally do its borrowing at the central bank, the proposal of supplementary requirements

---

[25] See George L. Bach, *Federal Reserve Policy Making* (New York: Alfred A. Knopf, 1950), p. 212. An illustration of this point is afforded by postwar experience with security-reserve requirements in Belgium. "The Belgian 'Banks with great circulation' are forced by law to invest more than 60 per cent of their short-term deposits in Treasury Certificates. In 1946, when this system was introduced, it helped to block the floating debt. Since then, the deposits have more than doubled so that the possibility for the Government to issue promissory notes has increased proportionately. If the Treasury spends the money and brings it into circulation it increases the deposits again, and so on.

"Thus the private sector of the economy is deprived of the possibility to have recourse to the banks for part of their financial needs by the latter's inability to lend. But a great deal of the monetary improvement, attained by this procedure, is lost again by the fact that the Government is supplied with easy money and consequently with a windfall opportunity to spend more. One cannot drive the economy with one foot on the accelerator of public expenditure and the other on the brake of credit restrictions." Leith-Ross, *op. cit.*, p. 18. Cf. Fousek, *op. cit.*, p. 68.

as an insulation device becomes irrelevant. With the Treasury borrowing directly from the central bank, such borrowing would in any event be insulated from the open market.[26]

It may be contended that supplementary security-reserve requirements are desirable as a halfway station to complete consolidation of fiscal and money-creating powers in the Treasury. However, those so contending should be quick to recall that, from the viewpoint of the Treasury's interest burden, the alternative of higher cash-reserve requirements is preferable to supplementary security-reserve requirements.

Finally, it is noteworthy that the exercise of monetary control is in itself quite complex and intricate even without being further encumbered with the problem of the interest cost of servicing Government debt. The national Government *qua* fiscal authority can, by means of tax policy, regulate the net interest cost of Government debt without saddling the central bank with this additional task. If, for example, the Government should wish to restrict the interest-income of commercial banks to some level lower than the one resulting from the Treasury's financing operations in the open market, the Government can tax commercial banks accordingly. Existence of the Government's taxing power permits determination of the nature of central-bank instruments to depend solely upon their efficacy in terms of monetary control rather than, additionally, upon fairness in terms of distributive justice.

[26] It is interesting that the two economists who have proposed direct borrowing by the Treasury from the Federal Reserve as a permanent arrangement have also stipulated that the Federal Reserve be permitted to deal in its own securities vis-à-vis the banks as well as the public (Bach, *op. cit.*, pp. 219-220, and Hart, *Defense and the Dollar*, pp. 183-185). Thus not even those in favor of the most thoroughgoing technique of insulating Treasury debt from the private economy have recommended that member banks be virtually barred from participation in open-market activity during periods of monetary tightness.

4

OPEN-MARKET OPERATIONS:

"BILLS-ONLY" DOCTRINE

AND ECONOMIC

STABILIZATION

I. CHOICE OF SECTOR

The central-bank technique of open-market operations has, in recent years, been the subject of growing attention and controversy. Should the monetary authority confine its open-market operations to one particular sector of the Government securities market or should it at times operate in more than one sector? Does it matter, in terms of central-bank influence on the level of economic activity, whether open-market operations take place in one sector of the market to the exclusion of others? If of little importance for central-bank influence on the level of economic activity, does the locus of open-market operations matter in terms of some other objectives of central banking?

In the United States these and related questions have been of particular interest, indeed concern, since the Federal Reserve Open Market Committee adopted in 1953 the so-called "bills-only" doctrine. Under this policy, open-market operations by the

Federal Reserve are generally to be confined to short-term securities, preferably Treasury bills. The "bills-only" doctrine is probably the most important innovation in the technique of monetary control utilized by the Federal Reserve subsequent to its 1951 accord with the Treasury, which restored the freedom of action of the central bank in open-market operations.

The controversial character of this innovation is readily illustrated by replies of 615 American university economists in 1958 to a questionnaire on economic policy prepared by the Joint Economic Committee of the United States Congress. To the question "Do you believe that 'tight money' served to dampen inflation during 1955-57?" the answer "Yes" was given by 74.6 per cent of the respondents.[1] Thus, it appears that a great majority of the respondents was not inclined to underestimate the general effectiveness of restrictive Federal Reserve policy. Yet from this general acknowledgment of the efficacy of restrictive Federal Reserve policy there did not follow affirmation of the potency of the "bills-only" policy in particular. To the phrase "In using open-market operations to influence long-term interest rates," only 7.5 per cent of the respondents thought that it would be correct to add that "Federal Reserve authorities should limit themselves exclusively (except in correcting 'disorderly markets') to purchase and sale of Treasury bills."[2] By contrast as many as 85.0 per cent of the respondents indicated that it would be correct to add that "Federal Reserve authorities should follow a flexible policy as regards securities dealt in, varying the types as circumstances may require."[3]

No less remarkable is the extent of agreement among members of the Open Market Committee itself on the propriety of the "bills-only" doctrine. In every instance in which adherence to this doctrine was put to a Committee vote, all members but one

[1] United States Congress, Joint Economic Committee, *Economic Policy Questionnaire*, 85th Congress, 2nd Session (Washington, D. C.: U. S. Government Printing Office, 1959), p. 6.

[2] *Ibid.*, p. 7.

[3] *Ibid.*

voted approval. Thus, university economists have been as close to unanimity in one direction as the Open Market Committee has been in the opposite direction. But the identity of the one dissenting member of the Committee is as noteworthy as the near unanimity on this issue, for that member is the president of the Federal Reserve Bank of New York (also Vice Chairman of the Open Market Committee), who is in charge of the institution that is the sole administrator of the entire System's open-market operations. The dissent of the New York Bank president has not been a total negation of the "bills-only" doctrine; rather, it has called for the qualification that "as a general rule" System open-market operations be confined to short-term securities.[4]

In this chapter, we examine the problem of technique in open-market operations from two points of view. In the first place, we consider the problem theoretically, i.e., from the viewpoint of the theory of the term structure of interest rates. Second, we explore the problem empirically, namely, from the viewpoint of the crisis-like behavior of the United States Government securities market during 1958. Though directly referring only to one particular monetary system in one particular period, the empirical analysis is intended as an illustration, or case study, of the general problem of technique in open-market operations as it may confront any monetary system with open-market operations in an extensive Government securities market.

II. THEORIES OF INTEREST-RATE STRUCTURE

Fundamental to analysis of the choice of open-market technique by the central bank is the theory of the term structure of interest rates. For, in the nature of the problem, any appraisal

---

4 See, for example, Board of Governors of the Federal Reserve System, *Annual Report for 1958* (Washington, D. C.: 1959), p. 40. It is noteworthy that the dissenting vote of the Federal Reserve Bank of New York has been cast by two successive bank presidents.

or prescription of open-market technique for the central bank necessarily implies some notions regarding the structure of interest rates.

At least four distinct types of theory of interest-rate structure have been expounded in the economic literature of recent decades.

One of these, which may be termed the fluidity theory of the structure of interest rates, was developed as an explanation of the behavior of American and British money markets during the 1920s.[5] In this theory, the markets for debts of different maturity are characterized by a fluidity of pressures from one market to another. Accordingly, though compartmentalized, these markets exhibit a correspondence, both in respect to direction and to timing, of movement of interest rates, with short-term rates moving proportionately more than long-term rates.

A logical inference from the fluidity theory, explicitly drawn by one of its authors, is that direct central-bank action upon short-term rates of interest has its influence readily transmitted to other interest rates.[6] Yet this inference is not drawn without qualification. When a slump occurs in bond prices, open-market operation in short-term securities may not be an efficient technique for reducing bond yields. For,

> circumstances can arise when, for a time, the natural rate of interest falls so low that there is a very wide and quite unusual gap between the ideas of borrowers and of lenders in the market on long-term. When prices are falling, profits low, the future uncertain and financial sentiment depressed and alarmed, the natural-rate of interest may fall, for a short period, almost to nothing. But it is precisely at such a time as this that lenders are most exigent and least inclined to embark their resources on long-term unless it be on the most unexceptionable security; so that the bond rate, far from falling towards nothing, may be expected—apart from the opera-

[5] See Winfield W. Riefler, *Money Rates and Money Markets in the United States* (New York: Harper and Brothers, 1930), pp. 5-9, 112-123; and John Maynard Keynes, *Treatise on Money*, ii (New York: Harcourt, Brace and Company, 1930), pp. 352-364.

[6] Keynes, *op. cit.*

tions of the Central Bank—to be higher than normal. How is it possible in such circumstances, we may reasonably ask, to keep the market-rate and the natural-rate of long-term interest at an equality with one another, *unless we impose on the Central Bank the duty of purchasing bonds up to a price far beyond what it considers to be the long-period norm.*[7]

In a recession or depression, therefore, direct operation in the long-term sector may be quite advantageous.

A second theory, which may be termed the "psychological" theory, is in a sense a generalization of the above-quoted qualification to the fluidity theory. The "psychological" (or "Keynesian") theory was developed as an explanation of the remarkable downward stickiness of long-term interest rates in the face of a sizable decline in short-term rates during the depression of the 1930s. According to this theory, the long-term rate is a "highly psychological" or "highly conventional phenomenon," dominated by short-run expectations regarding its future level.[8] Hence, there is little hope for exerting appreciable influence upon the long-term rate by means of operations in short-term debt alone. Particularly in times of declining business activity, even vigorous open-market purchases of short-term securities may fail to alter expectations regarding the long-term rate. Accordingly, "Where . . . (as in the United States, 1933-1934) open-market operations have been limited to the purchase of very short-dated securities, the effect may, of course, be mainly confined to the very short-term rate of interest and have but little reaction on the much more important long-term rates of interest."[9]

A third theory, which has been termed the expectational theory, states that the long-term interest rate tends to equal the

[7] *Ibid.*, pp. 372-373.

[8] John Maynard Keynes, *The General Theory of Employment, Interest and Money* (New York: Harcourt, Brace and Company, 1936), pp. 202-203. Reference to the psychological theory as "Keynesian" should be qualified as "Keynesian" in the sense of Keynes's *General Theory*. For the fluidity theory is also "Keynesian" but in the sense of Keynes's *Treatise on Money*.

[9] *Ibid.*, p. 197.

average of the expected short-term interest rates over the duration of the long-term debt.[10] Thus, long-term rates depend upon
the public's long-term expectations. Therefore, to be effective in
influencing long-term rates, the monetary authority may have to
engage in open-market operations in the long-term sector directly.[11]

Finally and most recently, there has been provided what may
be termed a substitutability theory of the term structure of interest rates, which is most akin to the fluidity theory of the
1920s.[12] Underscoring the substitutability between short-term
and long-term debt on the part of both borrowers and lenders,
the substitutability theory points to the coincidence in direction
and timing of movement of different rates as an expression of
the simultaneous impact of changes in general credit conditions
upon the various sectors of the money and capital markets. Yet
the substitutability between short-term and long-term debt is
found to be limited. With a substantial change in the maturity
structure of debt supplied to the economy, due either to debt
management operations by the Treasury or to actions of private
borrowers, the rate structure itself will alter. But behavior based
upon interest-rate expectations is important only as a factor of
short-run movements in long-term rates: the influence of expectations is not significant in determining interest-rate relation-
ships over considerable stretches of time.

As one would anticipate, the policy implications of the substitutability theory are most akin to those of the fluidity theory.
"Direct government action in debt markets is not ordinarily necessary to produce roughly simultaneous upward and downward
movements of long-term and short-term interest rates in response

10 John R. Hicks, *Value and Capital*, 2nd Edition (Oxford: Clarendon
Press, 1946), pp. 141-152, 260-262; and Friedrich A. Lutz, "The Structure
of Interest Rates," *Quarterly Journal of Economics*, LV (November 1940),
36-63.

11 Lutz, *op. cit.*, p. 60.

12 John M. Culbertson, "The Term Structure of Interest Rates," *Quarterly
Journal of Economics*, LXXI (November 1957), 485-517.

to business conditions and in monetary policy (assuming debt management policies of at least some minimum degree of appropriateness)."[13] A situation not considered "ordinary" is that of "the abnormal rate structure of the earlier 1930's."[14] Specifically, "What is truly singular about the behavior of the rate structure during the 1930's is the fact that long-term rates did not show larger declines during the earlier part of the period. It was four years before long-term rates began to show a full response to the remarkable drop in short-term rates in 1930. An effective program for economic stabilization cannot tolerate such a lag."[15]

Now two propositions are included in all four of the foregoing theories. Each theory either states or implies (a) that short-term rates fluctuate over a wider range than long-term rates; and (b) that, under some circumstances and for at least brief periods, there may be a lack of response of long-term rates to central-bank operations directly involving only short-term debt.

One need not count on an eventual settlement of the differences among the various theories to recognize that none of them sanctions a persistent avoidance of open-market operations in long-term securities as a means of influencing long-term rates. Indeed, the psychological and expectational theories have served as bases for rejection of a doctrine that would limit open-market operations by the central bank to short-term securities. And the fluidity theory, as well as the substitutability theory, though stressing the interconnection among debt markets, includes cognizance of variations in the fluidity of funds from one debt market to another. In other words, neither the fluidity theory nor the substitutability theory maintains that the speed of transmission of changes in general credit conditions among all debt markets is the same over the business cycle.

To be sure, in view of the institutional framework of debt-management operations in the United States, one can always

---

[13] *Ibid.*, p. 516.
[14] *Ibid.*
[15] *Ibid.*, pp. 513-514.

argue that even if the Federal Reserve strictly adhered to operations in short-term securities only, such a course would not necessarily curtail the effectiveness of monetary policy. To illustrate, if long-term rates remain sticky in the face of a sharp decline in short-term rates, an adherent of the substitutability theory might argue that the Treasury ought to bring about a substantial contraction in the maturity structure of Government debt, with the Federal Reserve continuously adhering to operations in short-term securities only. Such an argument, however, is at best a play on words and at worst a subterfuge for begging the issue. Open-market operations remain open-market operations whether the Treasury or the Federal Reserve carries them out. To suggest that the Treasury should manipulate the maturity structure of Government debt in a manner that would permit the Federal Reserve to limit its operations to short-term securities amounts to no more than shifting the burden of the problem of open-market technique from one Governmental institution to another.

III. THE RATIONALE FOR THE "BILLS-ONLY" DOCTRINE

Now the Federal Reserve System's "bills-only" doctrine includes recognition of a situation that may call for intervention in the markets for Government securities that are other than short term. The situation has been called one of "disorderly markets" and it is only for "correcting" such a situation that the System imposes on itself the obligation to deviate from the self-limitation to operations in short-term securities.[16] "Disorderly market conditions" have been described by the Federal Reserve as

a situation in which selling "feeds on itself," that is, a situation in which a fall in prices, instead of eliciting an increase in the amount of securities demanded and a decrease in the amount

16 See, for example, Board of Governors of the Federal Reserve System, *Annual Report for 1958*, p. 40.

supplied, elicits the reverse—a falling away of bids and a rise in both the number and the size of offerings. Temporarily there is no price level which will clear the market . . . .

In general, three conditions would have to exist to justify a finding of disorder: Spiralling price changes that tend to "feed upon themselves"; a trading vacuum accompanied by a buildup in the number and size of offerings and by a disappearance in bids; and a disorganized market psychology. The emergence of such conditions might be caused by or be coincident with major international or domestic political developments or a Treasury financing operation, although market disorder could conceivably develop in the absence of such external influence. This definition, is necessarily, general rather than precise; a determination that disorder exists in a particular market situation must rest upon appraisal of the combination of circumstances at the time, rather than upon application of firm criteria.[17]

From the foregoing quotation it is amply clear that the Federal Reserve's conception of "disorder" does not apply to a situation which, rather than involving a downward spiraling of prices (mounting of interest rates), is marked by a stickiness of long-term rates concomitant with a sharp decline of short-term rates. It follows that such a situation constitutes, under the "bills-only" doctrine, no ground for direct Federal Reserve intervention in security markets that are other than short term. Yet one policy implication that appears to be common to all four of the above-reviewed theories of the interest-rate structure is that when long-term rates show no appreciable response to a substantial reduction of short-term rates brought about by central-bank operations, direct official intervention in long-term markets is in order. What, then, are the theoretical foundations underlying the Federal Reserve's "bills-only" doctrine?

Two quite distinct explanations have been given by the Federal Reserve for the propriety of the "bills-only" doctrine. The first explanation, dating back to November 1952, constituted the

17 In United States Congress, Joint Economic Committee, *Employment, Growth, and Price Levels: Hearings,* Part 6A, 86th Congress, 1st Session (Washington, D. C.: U. S. Government Printing Office, 1959), pp. 1278-1279.

rationale for adoption of the doctrine and abandonment of the pre-existing policy of the Open Market Committee. The second explanation, issued in November 1958, constituted the rationale for continued adherence to the doctrine after the crisis-like behavior of the Government Securities market in mid-1958.

The 1952 explanation was given with reference to the behavior of the Government securities market during the twenty months subsequent to the Treasury-Federal Reserve Accord of March 1951.[18] The Accord had freed the Federal Reserve from commitment to a particular structure or level of interest rates on Government securities. In its ensuing experience with the Government securities market, the Federal Reserve deemed it essential to its open-market operations that "the inside market, i.e., the market that is reflected on the order books of specialists and dealers" must have "depth, breadth, and resiliency."[19]

"Depth" exists when "there are orders, either actual orders or orders that can be readily uncovered, both above and below the market."[20] "Breadth" exists "when these orders are in volume and come from widely divergent investor groups."[21] "Resiliency" exists "when new orders pour promptly into the market to take advantage of sharp and unexpected fluctuations in prices."[22]

Now the Federal Reserve Subcommittee that provided the 1952 explanation found that there prevailed a lack of depth, breadth, and resiliency in all issues of Government securities other than Treasury bills. In the light of its study of the testimony of Government security dealers, the Subcommittee concluded that the Open Market Committee was partly liable for

[18] Federal Open Market Committee Report of Ad Hoc Subcommittee on the Government Securities Market, November 12, 1952, published in United States Congress, Joint Committee on the Economic Report, *United States Monetary Policy: Recent Thinking and Experience: Hearings,* 83rd Congress, 2nd Session (Washington, D. C.: U. S. Government Printing Office, 1954), pp. 257-286.

[19] *Ibid.,* p. 265.

[20] *Ibid.*

[21] *Ibid.*

[22] *Ibid.*

lack of the qualities essential to the proper functioning of the Government securities market. This liability was due to the fact that, while claiming to be working toward a "free" market for Government securities in place of the rigid support of bond prices during the ten years preceding the Treasury-Federal Reserve Accord, the Open Market Committee continued to commit itself, both in word and in deed, to the "maintenance of orderly markets." To the actual and potential participants in the market, such a commitment implied capricious intervention, "official mothering" of the market. In the face of the Federal Reserve's bewildering inconsistency between formal pronouncements favoring a free market and actual measures of direct intervention in the market, dealers refrained from taking positions in volume and from making markets in intermediate- and long-term securities. Accordingly, it was the judgment of the Subcommittee that

the lack of professional dealer confidence in the intentions of the Federal Open Market Committee is justified, and that it is not enough for the development of an adequate market that the Committee's intervention be held to a strict minimum. It is important that the dealers be assured, if it is at all possible to give such assurance, that the Committee is prepared to permit a really free market in United States Government securities to develop without direct intervention for the purpose of establishing particular prices, yields, or patterns of yields.[23]

Thus, the "bills-only" doctrine arose out of the Federal Reserve's concern for the development of a securities market with depth, breadth, and resiliency, as a means of enhancing the effectiveness of open-market operations. In order to bring about the desired technical improvement of the market, it was deemed essential to reduce dealer uncertainty about intentions of the Open Market Committee. In the view of the Federal Reserve, this called for abstention, except for the correction of disorderly market conditions, from open-market operations in intermediate- and long-term securities.

[23] *Ibid.*, p. 267.

It is noteworthy that the Federal Reserve's rationale for adopting the "bills-only" doctrine includes little, if any, cognizance of a theory of term structure of interest rates. The one apparent exception to this statement is the following Subcommittee observation concerning fluctuations in the securities market that are neither self-correcting nor reflective of basic changes in the credit outlook. Of such fluctuations, states the Subcommittee, "the great preponderance, throughout all sectors of the market, will respond readily to arbitrage induced by positive intervention on the part of the Committee in the very short sector of the market. In other words, it is only rarely that selling creates a sufficiently disorderly situation to require intervention in other than the very short market."[24] Though expressing a clear notion about the strength of arbitrage, this quoted observation hardly approaches a theory of the structure of interest rates. The disorderly condition on which it is focused is one involving a pressure for yields to rise. Completely ignored, not only in this quotation but through the Subcommittee explanation, is the situation in which *declining* yields in the short-term market fail to elicit a decline of yields in intermediate and long-term markets. In other words, consideration of the possible behavior of interest rates during a severe recession or depression is entirely lacking. It is interesting that what little support the "bills-only" doctrine has been accorded in recent economic literature has been with the emphasis that the 1952 rationale of the doctrine is inextricably bound up with conditions of "tight money."[25] But this principal point of defense of the 1952 explanation highlights the severe limitation of its theoretical underpinning: the "bills-only" doctrine was adopted without regard to the behavior of interest rates under conditions other than those of "tight money."

24 *Ibid.*, p. 268.
25 David I. Fand and Ira O. Scott, Jr., "The Federal Reserve System's 'Bills Only' Policy: A Suggested Interpretation," *Journal of Business*, xxxi (January 1958), 17.

In November 1958 the Federal Reserve published a reappraisal of the "bills-only" doctrine in the light of its experience in the intervening years and with special attention to the first half of 1958 culminating in the disorderly conditions of the Government securities market in July 1958.[26] The 1958 reappraisal is similar to the 1952 Subcommittee report in one important respect: both conclude with espousal of the "bills-only" doctrine. But there the similarity ends. The 1958 explanation of the continued adherence to the "bills-only" doctrine is essentially different from the 1952 rationale for its adoption.

In reviewing the Federal Reserve's experience with implementation of the "bills-only" doctrine, the 1958 explanation says nothing by way of confirmation or refutation of the 1952 rationale for adoption of the doctrine, namely: improving the technical behavior of the Government securities market in the sense of augmenting its depth, breadth, and resiliency through inducing dealers to enlarge their positions in intermediate- and long-term securities. Rather, the 1958 explanation is designed to refute the criticism of the "bills-only" doctrine "on the grounds that it prevented the system from directly stimulating or restricting the volume of funds available to the long-term money markets."[27] In the course of this refutation, there emerges from the 1958 explanation a distinct theory of the term structure of interest rates, namely: the substitutability theory.

Thus, there is found to exist "a high degree of substitutability of security instruments . . . for many lenders and many borrowers in the credit and capital markets."[28] The factors of this "broad substitutability on both sides of the money and capital markets are more fundamental than arbitrage in accounting for

[26] Winfield W. Riefler (at the time, Assistant to the Chairman, Board of Governors of the Federal Reserve System), "Open Market Operations in Long-Term Securities," *Federal Reserve Bulletin*, XLIV (November 1958), 1260-1274.

[27] *Ibid.*, p. 1260.

[28] *Ibid.*, p. 1265.

the fluidity, homogeneity, and responsiveness of the securities market. This flexibility links the various sectors of the money and capital markets into a somewhat loosely integrated whole in which yield changes tend to move together in the various sectors."[29] Yet the coincidence of movement of different interest rates is by no means perfect. Consider a market transaction in Government securities. "The price or interest rate response to the change in market supply is registered most strongly on the particular issues that are bought or sold," even though the change "will also be reflected to some degree throughout all maturity sectors of the market by reason of actual or anticipated substitution and arbitrage in the market."[30]

To be sure, it is a "fact that changes in the tone or direction of the money markets that appear first in the bill sector of the Government securities market soon spread to the other sectors."[31] But this fact does not seem to apply as neatly to the situation of ease in bank reserves, i.e., recession or depression, as it applies to the situation of tightness in reserve positions. "Ease in reserve positions will not be quickly reflected in an increase in commercial bank investment in the long-term capital markets if banks generally are concerned about an insufficiency of short-term liquid assets or a high loan-deposit ratio. Under either condition, time is needed before bank activity in long-term investments is likely to be affected."[32]

The word "needed" is the key to the policy inference drawn by the Federal Reserve from the foregoing quotation. From the substitutability theory, as applied to a situation of ease in reserve positions, the Federal Reserve does not draw the inference that what is "needed" is action on its part to increase the speed with which changes in interest rates are transmitted during a recession from the short-term sector to other sectors. Instead, "time" is

29 *Ibid.*
30 *Ibid.*, p. 1262.
31 *Ibid.*, p. 1266.
32 *Ibid.*

what, according to the Federal Reserve, is "needed," i.e., patience by the public and by the Federal Reserve with the response of the long-term market. Such, at least, seems to be the drift of the following argument in the 1958 explanation.

> It takes time for banks to improve their liquidity by investing fresh accretions of reserves in liquid assets. As they do, rates in the short-term open money markets will tend to fall. It also takes time for borrowers, such as finance companies with access to short-term open markets, to refinance through these markets to repay bank loans, an operation that would bring about an improvement, that is, a reduction, in bank loan-deposit ratios.
>
> The time taken for these two processes to operate sometimes accounts for what may seem to be a sluggish response in the long-term markets to changes in the availability of funds in the short-term markets. Time for these adjustments to take place is indispensable when net free reserves have increased but liquidity in bank earning assets is low. Long-term markets will not respond until bank portfolios have become more liquid and banks are again in a position to extend direct support to long-term issues. The banks would need this time interval before extending such support even if the Federal Reserve System itself operated in the long end of the market.[33]

Nowhere in the 1958 explanation has it been recognized that to wait out the time that the banks "need" may mean to let a recession gather momentum. Nor has it been recognized that rapid direct support to the long-term market by the *central* bank may obviate any "need" for time before *commercial* banks are "again in a position to extend direct support to long-term issues." Indeed, the *raison d'etre* of a central bank would be subject to serious doubt if the central bank were, as a matter of policy, willing to let a recession deepen while commercial banks were having their "need" for time satisfied.

Other observations contained in the 1958 explanation likewise fail to harmonize with the "bills-only" doctrine. Thus, in line with the substitutability theory of the structure of interest rates, the 1958 explanation reiterates the view that the effects of be-

[33] *Ibid.*

havior based upon interest-rate expectations are only short run.
Yet, for the short-run stretch, such effects are not negligible.
On the contrary, "when System actions give rise to firm expectations among market professionals with respect to interest rate
trends, relatively small System operations may have important
short-run effects on market quotations."[34] For

> at times these quotations may reflect professional expectations
> fully as much as or more than they do changes either in the
> reserve positions of the banks or in the amount of market-held
> securities in the various maturity sectors. This factor could
> become still more important if open-market operations were
> conducted in the intermediate or long sector of the market. It
> is most likely to be minimized when open market operations
> are confined to the bill sector.[35]

Here then, on the basis of its operating experience since the
Treasury-Federal Reserve Accord of 1951, the Federal Reserve
identifies an important, albeit short-term, influence of open-
market operations in the intermediate or long sector of the securities market. In view of the generally recognized fact that monetary policy is commonly less effective in counteracting reces-
sionary forces than in curbing inflationary pressures, the logical
inference from the foregoing quotation is clearly not that the independent influence on interest rates exerted by the central bank
via market expectations ought to be minimized even in a recession. Surely, the logically correct inference would be, rather,
that in that phase of the business cycle when monetary policy is,
in any case, relatively ineffective, the central bank ought to be
particularly eager to use the tools at its command to the maximum of their potency. Consequently, in times of recession, the
central bank should seize, rather than reject, the opportunity to
conduct open-market operations in the intermediate- and long-
term sectors of the securities market.

This last conclusion is supported not only by the Federal Reserve's own operating experience, as reflected in the 1958 ex-

34 *Ibid.*, p. 1263.
35 *Ibid.*, p. 1270.

planation, but by the literature on the responsiveness of economic activity to changes in interest rates. One definite result from the analysis of the interest elasticity of investment demand is that investment of high longevity, particularly in public utilities, has been found to be highly interest elastic.[36] Outlays of manufacturing firms for plant and equipment also appear to be affected by interest rates.[37] During 1949-1959 approximately one quarter of all business expenditures for new plant and equipment occurred in transportation and public utilities.[38] In making decisions concerning such high-longevity investment it is, of course, long-term interest rates that are relevant. In view of the role of investment in cyclical fluctuations, any measure enhancing the flexibility of long-term interest rates may be of more than negligible importance for the effectiveness of contra-cyclical policy. Insofar as it prevails, central-bank refusal to operate in long-term markets in times of recession lends support to the view that the Federal Reserve System "has been mistaken in its stubborn adherence to the bills' only doctrine. By surrendering the use of more widely dispersed open-market operations, the System has discarded an important means of control without gaining much in exchange."[39]

On the other hand, it has been contended that critics of the "bills-only" doctrine " have for the most part erected a strawman. They have taken the Federal Reserve System too literally in that they have criticized 'bills only' as a general theory of central

[36] See Lawrence R. Klein, "Studies in Investment Behavior," in National Bureau of Economic Research, *Conference on Business Cycles* (New York: N.B.E.R., 1951), pp. 233-303.

[37] See Franz Gehrels and Suzanne Wiggins, "Interest Rates and Manufacturers' Fixed Investment," *American Economic Review*, XLVII (March 1957), 79-92.

[38] See *Economic Report of the President*, January 1960 (Washington, D. C.: U. S. Government Printing Office, 1960), p. 190.

[39] Richard A. Musgrave in United States Congress, Joint Economic Committee, *Employment, Growth, and Price Levels: Hearings*, Part 8, 86th Congress, 1st Session (Washington, D. C.: U. S. Government Printing Office, 1959), p. 2766.

banking, when, in our view, the System had in mind only a tactic in the specific context of the post-Accord bond market."[40] This latter view is based on the explicit prediction that "in the event of a serious decline in employment, 'bills only' would be rejected with dispatch. In order to prevent a liquidity crisis, the Federal Reserve System would buy aggressively at long, as well as short, maturity levels."[41] Yet this prediction is not without some hedging, for "there remains the question whether the ability of the central bank to recognize a situation that requires action in the long-term sector will be hampered by the existence of the doctrine. This, and not the possibility that the Federal Reserve System would use 'bills only' in a situation where it was *clearly* inappropriate, is perhaps the main shortcoming of the policy."[42]

On second reading, the last quotation turns out to be self-contradictory: insofar as the "bills-only" doctrine impairs the ability of the central bank to recognize a situation calling for action in the long-term sector, the doctrine will be used in a situation where it is clearly inappropriate.

IV. THE EARLY 1958 EXPERIENCE

In order to find out the extent to which the "bills-only" doctrine is apt to impair the central bank's ability to recognize a situation calling for operations in the long-term sector, it is useful to consider the conduct of open-market operations in the first half of 1958. Not only did those months include the sharpest recession in the American economy since 1945, but the behavior of the Government securities market leading up to the disorderly condition of July 1958 has been subjected to a detailed special study undertaken jointly by the Treasury and the

[40] Fand and Scott, *op. cit.*, p. 18.
[41] *Ibid.*, p. 17.
[42] *Ibid.*, p. 18.

Federal Reserve System.[43] It is, therefore, possible to focus on a critical period for open-market operations with the aid of a particularly informative factual review of the unfolding of developments that have been of profound concern to the central bank as well as to other parts of the Government and the public.

For more than two years prior to October 1957, a policy of restraint on credit expansion had been pursued by the Federal Reserve System. As late as August 1957 discount rates at Federal Reserve Banks had risen to their postwar peak of 3.5 per cent, and net borrowed reserves had been in the range of $400-$500 million from April 1957 into October 1957.

By late October 1957 the System began to respond to the clearly emerging picture of a reversal in the cyclical upswing of 1954-1957. This response involved a moderate easing in the reserve position of member banks, brought about through System open-market operations in late October and early November. More conspicuously, in mid-November discount rates at Federal Reserve Banks were reduced from the peak of 3.5 per cent to 3.0 per cent.

Market reaction to the reduction of discount rates was swift and strong: there occurred an abrupt turnabout in market expectations regarding the direction of monetary policy. Widely interpreted as the forerunner in a series of anti-recession measures on the part of the monetary authority, the discount-rate reduction was quickly followed by a break in market interest rates, long as well as short. As indicated in Table 3, between October 1957 and January 1958, the drop in market yields was nearly .50 percentage points on long-term Government bonds and 1.14 on three-month Treasury bills.

After January, however, the pattern of decline in Government security yields changed drastically. While short-term rates continued to drop substantially until June, long-term rates moved

[43] See particularly *Part II: Factual Review for 1958* of the *Treasury-Federal Reserve Study of the Government Securities Market* (Washington, D. C.: February 1960).

TABLE 3.   *Market Yields of U. S. Government Securities*

(Per cent per annum)

Year and month	3-month bills	9- to 12-month issues	3- to 5-year issues	Bonds, 10 or more years to maturity
1957: September	3.53	4.02	3.93	3.66
October	3.58	3.94	3.99	3.73
November	3.29	3.52	3.63	3.57
December	3.04	3.09	3.04	3.30
1958: January	2.44	2.56	2.77	3.24
February	1.54	1.93	2.67	3.26
March	1.30	1.77	2.50	3.25
April	1.13	1.35	2.33	3.12
May	.91	1.21	2.25	3.14
June	.83	.98	2.25	3.19
July	.91	1.34	2.54	3.36
August	1.69	2.14	3.11	3.60
September	2.44	2.84	3.57	3.75

Source: *Federal Reserve Bulletin,* XLIV (October 1958), 1189.

slightly up and down to a June level that was little below that
of January. Thus, as shown in Table 3, between January 1958
and June 1958 the drop in market yields on three-month bills
was by virtually two-thirds, whereas on long-term bonds the reduction was by less than two-hundredths.

The result of this asymmetrical movement was, as illustrated
on Chart I, a sharp change in the structure of interest rates
from the fall of 1957 to mid-1958. The yield spread between
short-term and long-term securities widened greatly due to "the
fact that, after the initial sharp drop in late 1957, yields on
medium- and long-term bonds had not declined as usual relative
to short-term interest rates as in other periods of recession in
the past."[44] By the end of May 1958, as indicated on Chart I,
the yield spread between short-term and long-term securities
widened to more than 2.5 percentage points.

[44] *Ibid.,* p. 28.

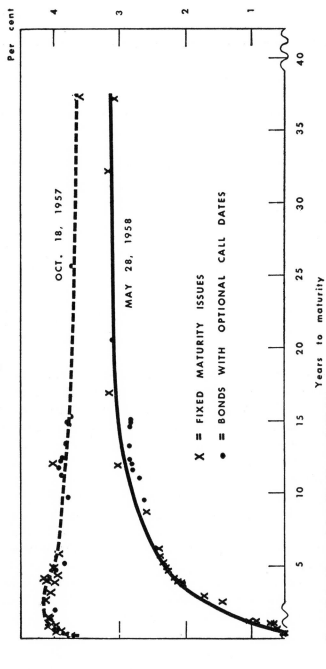

YIELD CURVES — U. S. GOVERNMENT SECURITIES

Per cent

OCT. 18, 1957

MAY 28, 1958

X = FIXED MATURITY ISSUES

● = BONDS WITH OPTIONAL CALL DATES

Years to maturity

Source: Federal Reserve Bulletin, XLIV (October 1958), 1189.

The downward stickiness of long-term rates throughout the first half of 1958 prevailed in the face of a series of expansionary monetary measures which—as the market had expected—followed on the heels of the discount-rate reduction of mid-November 1957. From a pre-November range of $400-$500 million of net borrowed reserves member banks were led by the System to a position of free reserves by year-end, and thence to a level of free reserves of about $500 million by March, a level maintained through July. All three of the major instruments of central banking were used by the System to this end. Between November 1957 and April 1958, there were four reductions in Federal Reserve Bank discount rates, from 3.50 per cent to 1.75 per cent. By means of three successive reserve-requirement reductions in early 1958, the Federal Reserve Board released about $1.5 billion of required bank reserves. And through open-market operations between November 1957 and June 1958, the System supplied commercial banks with an additional $2 billion of reserve funds.

What accounts for the stickiness of long-term rates in the face of the sharp decline in short-term rates concomitant with an expansionary monetary policy? And what significance, if any, is to be attributed to this stickiness? Response to these questions implies consideration of the demand for and the supply of funds, in the general framework of economic conditions during the 1957-1958 recession.

It is not only its severity in terms of total production and employment that differentiates the recession of 1957-1958 from the two preceding postwar recessions. The 1948-1949 episode had been essentially an inventory recession. The 1953-1954 downturn had been, in the main, an adjustment of the economy from defense to private spending following the end of the Korean war. The 1957-1958 recession, however, featured a large drop in business spending for fixed capital. Indeed, "The fact that economic recession from the autumn of 1957 to midspring 1958 involved heavy reduction in plant and equipment outlays (as well

TABLE 4. *Funds Raised in U. S. Capital Markets**

(In billions of dollars)

	1957				1958	
Type of Borrowing	1st Quarter	2nd Quarter	3rd Quarter	4th Quarter	1st Quarter	2nd Quarter
Corporate bonds and stocks . . .	3.4	3.1	2.9	3.0	3.1	2.6
State and local governments . . .	1.8	1.7	1.5	2.0	2.3	2.2
Foreign and international	.2	.2	.1	.1	.3	.5
Mortgages	5.6	6.2	6.4	6.0	5.3	6.4
Subtotal	11.0	11.2	10.9	11.1	11.0	11.7
U. S. Treasury	.0	.3	1.9	2.2	6.8	11.9
Total	11.0	11.5	12.8	13.3	17.8	23.6

*Offerings of long-term securities for new capital and nonfarm mortgage recordings of $20,000 or less. U. S. Treasury borrowings represent securities with maturities of 4¾ years or longer offered for cash or in exchange, excluding allotments to Treasury and Federal Reserve accounts.

Source: *Treasury-Federal Reserve Study of the Government Securities Market, Part II: Factual Review for 1958* (Washington, D. C.: February 1960), p. 9.

as more rapid inventory liquidation than in the two previous recessions), together with the speed of the decline, seemed to support the view that the recession was likely to be deeper and more protracted than anything the United States had experienced since the 1930's."[45]

Notwithstanding the substantial drop in plant outlays and the widespread apprehension of a further deepening of the recession, the demand for long-term funds in capital markets remained surprisingly large. As shown in Table 4, the total of non-Federal borrowings in long-term markets was slightly higher in the first half of 1958 than in the first half of 1957. Moreover, long-term borrowing by the Federal Government during the recession rose enormously. In consequence, total long-term borrowings were more than 80 per cent higher in the first half of 1958 than in the first half of 1957.

[45] *Ibid.*, p. 7.

By contrast, the demand for short-term borrowings drifted downward in the course of the recession. Of particular relevance to the drop in short-term rates on Government securities is the fact that between October and June there took place a substantial decline in the volume of short-term securities relative to long-term instruments.

On the supply side of funds, there was little increase in the flow of funds to capital markets from the major financial intermediaries (i.e., insurance companies, mutual savings banks, and savings and loan associations) in the first half of 1958 as compared with the first half of 1957. By far the largest source of an increase in the supply of funds was the commercial banking system, whose reserve position, as previously noted, was greatly eased between October 1957 and June 1958 under the impact of the Federal Reserve's expansionary policy. Of the total increase in loans and investments of commercial banks between October and June, more than half consisted of increased purchases of Federal Government securities, and a further two-fifths consisted of other securities. Thus, less than 20 per cent ($2 billion) of the increase in the supply of funds by commercial banks consisted of loans, mostly loans based on securities.

Sensitive to an unusually large October-to-June growth in demand deposits that were principally United States Government deposits, "Banks were naturally interested in investing these new demand deposits in intermediate- and short-term securities, especially the latter."[46] Reinforced by the lengthened maturity structure of marketable Government debt, "The quest of banks for short-term instruments . . . helped to depress short-term interest rates to low levels."[47] Accordingly, the behavior of commercial banks was still another factor in the widening of the yield spread between short-term and long-term instruments.

From October 1957 through June 1958, the Federal Reserve System strictly adhered to the "bills-only" doctrine. Accordingly,

[46] *Ibid.*, p. 17.
[47] *Ibid.*, p. 18.

System holdings of Treasury bills rose between late October and late June by more than $2 billion, while System holdings of all other Government securities declined slightly. It was not until the second half of July that, in the wake of news concerning the threat of war in the Middle East, the System deviated briefly from the "bills-only" doctrine to correct a "demoralized" condition in the Government securities market.[48] By the time of that deviation there had existed definitive evidence that economic recovery had been in progress for several weeks.

Thus, for at least four months—January through April—of the sharpest downturn in the American economy since World War II, the System avoided, as a matter of principle, operations in the intermediate- and long-term sectors of the open market. It pursued this principle in the face of stickiness of long-term yields concomitant with diminishing fixed investment. Not until a state of congestion in the bond market had reached crisis-like dimensions did the System countenance temporary deviation from the "bills-only" doctrine. At no earlier point does the System appear to have been deterred from limiting its open-market purchases to Treasury bills despite the acknowledged fact that the only significant source of an increase in the market's supply of funds during the recession—the commercial-banking system— was guided by a quest for short-term instruments while the volume of long-term instruments was rising vigorously.

Yet, having adhered to the "bills-only" doctrine in the first half of 1958, the System—as well as the Treasury—refrained in the study of the 1958 securities market from discussion of the "bills-only" doctrine. One may readily grant that limitation of the scope of the study was both necessary and desirable. Nevertheless, in what is supposed to be a study of factors underlying the crisis-like market behavior of 1958, it appears neither necessary nor desirable to ignore the contribution of the "bills-only" policy to the widening spread between short-term and long-term rates. Manifestly, System abstention from operations in the

48 See *ibid.*, pp. 81-83.

long-term market was an essential condition for the yield spread to have widened to the extent that it did.

V. "MINIMUM INTERVENTION"

The "bills-only" doctrine was adopted by the Federal Reserve System as part of a more general policy, the policy of minimum intervention by the central bank in the open market.[49] The 1958 recession, however, highlights a basic conflict between the "bills-only" doctrine on the one hand and the minimum-intervention objective on the other. Under the money market and capital market conditions of October 1957 to June 1958, the objective of minimum intervention would have called for direct intervention in the long-term market. For a larger reduction of long-term rates and a greater easing of credit availability in the long-term sector would have been effected through the same volume of central-bank purchases of long-term securities as the volume of purchases of short-term securities actually carried out by the Federal Reserve. Thus, adherence to the "bills-only" doctrine in times such as the 1958 recession means that the central bank is placed in a strait jacket that prevents it from pursuing the minimum-intervention objective. Rather than being a logical corollary of this objective, the "bills-only" doctrine turns out to be an impediment to it.

But the minimum-intervention objective itself is a dubious proposition on several counts.

In the first place, if interpreted literally, minimum intervention in the open market would imply that the central bank should avoid open-market operations so long as other tools of central banking can be used to bring about a particular desired change in banks' reserve position. Yet this interpretation conflicts with the System's own insistence that variations of cash-

49 Federal Open Market Committee Report of the Ad Hoc Subcommittee on the Government Securities Market, *op. cit.*, p. 266.

reserve requirements ought not usually to be used in place of open-market operations, even though both instruments can be used to the same effect in terms of banks' aggregate reserve position.[50] Hence, whatever "minimum intervention" means, to the System it means something clearly short of complete abstention from open-market operations.

Second, and more fundamental, the objective of minimum intervention was explicitly inferred by the System from the still higher objective of greater depth, breadth, and resiliency of the market for Government securities other than Treasury bills. It is seriously questionable, however, whether minimum intervention has, in fact, led to this higher objective. Indeed, the Federal Reserve Bank of New York has testified to the contrary.[51] In any event, Government security dealers have continued to eschew long positions in bonds as scrupulously as they had before adoption of the minimum-intervention policy. Recently, the very relevance of the depth-breadth-resiliency objective has been questioned. A recent study of the United States Government securities market finds that,

> It is difficult to understand why anybody should expect any market for large long-term instruments to be anything but thin. Under any circumstances the sensitivity of prices of long-term bonds to yield changes makes dealer type rather than brokerage type business highly risky. Without large dealer inventories, large blocks of bonds are necessarily hard to move. The demand for depth, breadth, and resiliency seems to stem from the use of bonds as liquidity rather than investment instruments. By their very nature long-term bonds are not satisfactory liquidity instruments. The attempt to attribute the deficiency to the market rather than the instrument itself seems somewhat unreasonable.[52]

[50] See Chapter II above.

[51] Allan Sproul (at the time, President of the Federal Reserve Bank of New York), in *United States Monetary Policy: Recent Thinking and Experience: Hearings*, pp. 226-227.

[52] Roland I. Robinson and Morris Mendelson, *The Market for United States Treasury Obligations* (New York: National Bureau of Economic Research, 1959, preliminary), Chapter VI, pp. 35-36.

Finally, whatever else "minimum intervention" means, the Federal Open Market Committee has voted that it does mean that open-market operations "shall not include offsetting purchases and sales of securities for the purpose of altering the maturity pattern of the System's portfolio."[53] Thus, "minimum intervention" precludes what is commonly referred to as a "swapping operation," i.e., a simultaneous purchase and sale by the System of securities of different maturities, leaving the System's total volume of securities unchanged but altering the composition of that volume. Since it leaves total System holdings unaffected, a swapping operation neither absorbs nor releases bank reserves: its net effect on bank reserves is zero. Hence, swapping operations are a means for altering the maturity structure of interest rates without tightening or easing bank reserves.

Now the prohibition of swapping operations rests on the notion that the effectiveness of central banking is maximized by measures that merely absorb or release bank reserves. This notion is negated by the lesson that emerges from the System's own recent experience as well as from the body of theory of the interest-rate structure.

That lesson is the occurrence of variations in the rapidity of the flow of funds from one sector of the credit market to another. On the upswing, as the demand for credit mounts in the face of a tightening reserve position of commercial banks, the fluidity of funds in response to market pressures heightens. On the downswing, when the quest of commercial banks for short-term debt is accompanied by a rise in long-term borrowing by the fiscal authorities, there is apt to be sluggishness of long-term rates concomitant with expansion of excess bank reserves.

Swapping operations permit the central bank to influence the long-term sector not only directly but also massively, without thereby releasing bank reserves on a scale that would constitute a potential for future inflation. By contrast, in the absence of

53 Board of Governors of the Federal Reserve System, *Annual Report for 1958*, p. 40.

swapping operations, direct and sizable support of the long-term, or any other, sector necessarily means the creation of an inflationary potential that may be quite in excess of what the central bank would wish to contemplate. Thus, having debarred itself from swapping operations, the central bank is handicapped in contributing to economic stability. The policy of "minimum intervention" appears to be a step toward reduced, if not minimum, central-bank effectiveness.

VI. INTERNATIONAL ASPECT

In conclusion, it is noteworthy that international monetary considerations also militate against confinement of open-market operations to the short end. Suppose that a country experiences a deficit in its balance of payments. This deficit accrues to other countries as a surplus of receipts from the deficit country. The other countries may use this surplus to build up deposits in the deficit country's currency, to acquire securities in the deficit country's money market, or to buy gold. The other countries have incentive to buy gold, rather than to accumulate short-term claims against the deficit country, if short-term interest rates in the deficit country are low relative to short-term interest rates abroad.[54]

Now assume that a recession occurs in the deficit country in the face of prosperity abroad, and that in order to counteract the recession, the central bank in the deficit country engages in an expansionary domestic policy. As previously noted, one important proposition regarding the maturity structure of interest rates is that the amplitude of fluctuations of short-term rates is greater than that of long-term rates. Therefore, expansionary open-

[54] See the highly suggestive analysis by Edward M. Bernstein, *International Effects of U. S. Economic Policy*, Study Paper No. 16 for United States Congress, Joint Economic Committee, 86th Congress, 2nd Session (Washington, D. C.: U. S. Government Printing Office, 1960), pp. 80-83.

market operations confined to the short-term sector will pull down domestic short-term rates relative to foreign short-term rates further than would open-market operations in other maturity sectors. And the wider the international differential in short-term rates, the greater will be the incentive for the other countries to use their surplus of receipts from the deficit country for buying gold instead of accumulating short-term claims. Thus, a drain of the international currency reserves of the deficit country will be precipitated or intensified by a "bills only" policy as contrasted with a more eclectic open-market policy. The sizable gold outflow from the United States in the course of the American recession during the second half of 1960 suggests that no central bank in an open economy—not even in the world's richest open economy—can afford to ignore the international differential in short-term rates to which its open-market policy contributes.

In brief, to operate on the reserve base of an economy's money supply is not always enough. The objective of international—as well as of domestic—economic stabilization also calls for central-bank preparedness to operate directly on the term structure of interest rates. Because it prevents such central-bank preparedness, the policy of confining open-market operations to the short-term sector is an impediment to economic stabilization at home and abroad.

5

BANK RATE,

REDISCOUNT RATE, AND

OTHER INTEREST RATES

I. INTRODUCTION

Discretionary control of the monetary system—i.e., central banking—is the product of a specific institutional setting. Both in its practice and in its theory, central banking has its origin in the activities of one particular institution: the Bank of England.[1]

The practice of central banking has a history of less than two centuries; and up to the twentieth century—when most central banks were founded—it was largely identifiable with the Bank of England. The theory of central banking received its impetus in Walter Bagehot's *Lombard Street,* an 1873 classic expounding the special role of the Bank of England as lender of last resort. Thus, one particular weapon of one particular central bank, i.e., the Bank Rate of the Bank of England, constituted the focus of initial development of the theory as well as practice of central banking. This prominence of Bank Rate is the more remarkable as "London has long been regarded as the classic money market for domestic needs, for international requirements, and for fur-

[1] See Richard S. Sayers, *Central Banking After Bagehot* (Oxford: Clarendon Press, 1957), pp. 1-19.

nishing the central bank with a suitable milieu in which to exert its influence with reasonable assurance of a prompt, sensitive, and general response."[2]

It is, therefore, quite understandable that when a system of central banking was established in the United States, under the Federal Reserve Act of 1913, discount rates of the Federal Reserve Banks were regarded as the principal instrument of monetary control. Not until 1922 did open-market operations come to be recognized in the United States as a tool of central banking. And not until 1933 did the variation of cash-reserve requirements come into existence as a further technique of American central banking.

The nature and functions of discount policy as a tool of monetary control can be illuminated by means of a comparison between its English and American versions.[3] Such a comparison contributes to the appraisal of the discount weapon in relation to other techniques of monetary control. Such a comparison also illustrates the extent to which particular techniques of monetary control may be affected, in terms of their relevance, nature, and implications, by institutional features that differ with time and place.

II. THE CONTRAST

(i) In the United States, borrowers from Federal Reserve Banks at the discount rate are commercial banks. In Britain, borrowers from the Bank of England at "Bank Rate" are not the commercial banks but the twelve London discount houses that form the London Discount Market Association.

[2] Robert V. Roosa, *Federal Reserve Operations in the Money and Government Securities Markets* (New York: Federal Reserve Bank of New York, 1956), p. 14.

[3] For a comprehensive survey of the contemporary British monetary system see Committee on the Working of the Monetary System (Radcliffe Committee), *Report* (London: Her Majesty's Stationery Office, 1959).

In the strict English institutional sense of the term "money market," the London discount houses make up the London money market. These discount houses are essentially an adjunct to the London clearing banks, the large branch-banking institutions that perform the bulk of Britain's commercial banking business. The principal activity of the discount houses is lending funds that they borrow, earning the difference between the lower rate they pay and the higher rate they receive. In very large part, their lending activity is as holders of Treasury bills and short-dated Government bonds (their holdings of commercial bills having dwindled in significance). Their borrowings are overwhelmingly from commercial banks on a call basis. Thus the discount houses are a buffer between the commercial-banking system and the Bank of England. Because it is to the discount houses alone that it serves as a lender of last resort, the Bank of England channels through the discount houses the marginal amounts of cash reserves with which it may choose to provide the commercial-banking system without resort to open-market operations.

(ii) Member-bank borrowing from Federal Reserve Banks is subject to "the principles of prudent discounting."[4] These principles include not only regulations regarding the instruments eligible for rediscounting, but guidelines for individual consideration of each application for reserve accommodation on its own merits. Specifically,

> In considering a request for credit accommodation, each Federal Reserve Bank gives due regard to the purpose of the credit and to its probable effects upon the maintenance of sound credit conditions, both as to the individual institution and the economy generally. It keeps informed of and takes into account the general character and amount of the loans and investments of the member bank. It considers whether the bank is borrowing principally for the purpose of obtaining a tax advantage or profiting from rate differentials and whether the bank is extending an undue amount of credit for the specu-

[4] Board of Governors of the Federal Reserve System, *Annual Report for 1957* (Washington, D. C.: 1958), p. 11.

lative carrying of or trading in securities, real estate, or commodities, or otherwise.[5]

On the other hand, discount-house borrowing from the Bank
of England is not regulated by "merits-of-the-case" considerations. Subject only to general regulations regarding the eligibil-
ity of the instruments to be rediscounted, the Bank of England
"will never refuse to lend."[6]

(iii) In periods of monetary restraint, the market rate for
overnight money tends to equal the discount rate at Federal Reserve Banks. Thus in terms of the interest charge, member banks
are not penalized by borrowing, when the money market is tight,
from the Federal Reserve rather than from alternative sources.

In contrast, the interest charge for discount-house borrowing
from the Bank of England is severe by comparison with the terms
on which discount houses normally borrow day-to-day funds in
the private credit market. Loans at the Bank of England's Discount Office are usually for a minimum period of seven days; and
Bank Rate is commonly anywhere from 1.00 to 1.75 per cent
above other day-to-day money rates. In other words, Bank Rate
is a penalty rate.

(iv) In the United States there has developed an active market of one-day reserve balances at Federal Reserve Banks: the
Federal-funds market.[7] This market affords member banks a
means of adjusting their reserve positions on a day-to-day basis
by bringing together member banks possessing excess reserves
with member banks facing a reserve deficiency. To the extent
that member banks can accommodate each other in meeting
their cash-reserve obligations, their dependence on borrowing
from the central bank is reduced. Thus the Federal-funds market provides an important alternative to the rediscount mecha-

[5] *Ibid.*, p. 10.

[6] Radcliffe Committee, *op. cit.*, p. 120.

[7] For a survey of the history and contemporary character of this market,
see Board of Governors of the Federal Reserve System, *The Federal Funds
Market: A Study by a Federal Reserve System Committee* (Washington,
D. C.: 1959).

nism. In a unit-banking system with some 13,000 independent banks, the emergence and development of a Federal-funds market is, at least in part, the analogue for the pooling of reserves that can take place among the branch offices of a single bank in a branch-banking system.

In the United Kingdom, branch banking is the dominant form in the commercial-banking business. This fact, reinforced by the ease with which the banks can call loans made to discount houses, must surely go a long way in accounting for the absence from the London scene of a market that is a direct counterpart of the American Federal-funds market.

(v) The relationship between the discount rate at Federal Reserve Banks and other market rates is a somewhat tenuous one. This seems to be an inevitable result of the Federal Reserve System's own conception of the role of the discount rate. In the words of the System's Board of Governors,

> Although effective discount policy requires that the discount rate remain in touch with market rates, there are no simple rules governing either the magnitude or timing of changes in discount rates. A given change in discount rates may in some circumstances express a shift in direction or intensity of policy. In other circumstances, however, a change may merely represent a technical adjustment designed to maintain the existing degree of restraint or ease, when variations in the strength of credit demands have caused market rates to move substantially above or below the prevailing discount rate.[8]

On balance, it appears that the role of the discount rate, since the Federal Reserve's return to an active discount policy in 1952, has been one of follower rather than leader in the movement of interest rates. Certainly in the case of the 1955-1957 period of monetary restraint, the Board itself has acknowledged that "In most instances, the advance in discount rates represented an adjustment to changes that had occurred in market rates rather than an attempt to lead market rates."[9]

[8] Board of Governors, *Annual Report for 1957*, p. 14.
[9] *Ibid.*, p. 17.

The conduct of Bank Rate contrasts sharply with that of Federal Reserve discount policy. The relationship between Bank Rate and other market rates is rather clearly in one direction: Bank Rate leads in the adjustment of other market rates, at least in the short-term sector. Short-term interest rates, particularly those charged by banks, appear to be anchored to Bank Rate.

III. IMPLICATIONS

The notion of the central bank as lender of last resort may have two quite different meanings. The original meaning of this notion is that advanced by Bagehot: in case of a financial panic, the central bank must stand ready to lend to the private economy in whatever volume necessary to counteract the panic.

Though intended as a guideline for the Bank of England, Bagehot's meaning is not the one followed by the Bank of England in the course of its actual subsequent performance as lender of last resort. The meaning expressed through the Bank Rate policy of the Bank of England is the willingness of the central bank to lend, at a penalty rate, to the private economy *at all times*. The charging of a penalty rate—a rate higher than market rates on comparable maturities—insures that recourse to the central bank's lending facilities will be a "last resort." But this is a meaning of "last resort" distinct from the much more limited one contributed by Bagehot, namely, the case of financial panic.

The discount policy of Federal Reserve Banks does not make them lenders of last resort under either meaning of this notion. Not only do Federal Reserve Banks lend at times other than those of financial panic but the discount rates they charge, as previously pointed out, are not commonly penalty rates. Indeed, under certain circumstances, Federal Reserve Banks approach what might be termed a position of lenders of first resort. Thus, in conditions of monetary tightness, the Federal-funds rate will rise to the level of the discount rate but will not exceed that level.[10] In other words, the level of the discount rate acts as a ceiling upon the Federal-funds rate. This, in turn, means that in times of strong demand for private credit concomitant with a restrictive central-bank policy, it is more profitable for member banks to resort to the discount window of Federal Reserve Banks than to bid up the Federal-funds rate.

It is, therefore, hardly surprising that since 1952 there has occurred, as indicated in Table 5, a veritable revival of utilization of the discount mechanism in the United States, following nearly a generation (1934-1952) of little use of this facility. The revival coincided with a return to an active anti-inflationary monetary policy on the part of the central bank. In the ensuing general rise of interest rates, resort to borrowing from the central bank swiftly became attractive to member banks in spite of a rise in the discount rate itself. So long as the discount rate is not a penalty rate, why should member banks act otherwise than increase their borrowing when the demand for credit is strong and the central bank is engaged in restrictive open-market operations? Like anyone else, commercial bankers might as well make hay while the sun shines.

Nor is it surprising that the fluctuations that have occurred in the volume of rediscounting since the revival of this facility have been cyclical in character, the volume varying, as shown in Table 5, from $100 million in a recession to about $1 billion in a boom. In the words of the Chairman of the Federal Reserve Board,

> Variation in total volume of member-bank borrowing that occurs over the business cycle results from the fact, that at times of strong or expanding credit demands and restrictive monetary

[10] Not since 1928-1929 has the Federal-funds rate risen above the discount rate. See Board of Governors of the Federal Reserve System. *The Federal Funds Market,* pp. 28-29.

TABLE 5.

Member-Bank Borrowings in the United States, 1950-1959

	Total member-bank borrowings from all Federal Reserve Banks in millions of dollars and by quarterly averages of daily indebtedness	Discount rate at Federal Reserve Bank of New York in per cent per annum
1950: I	95	1½
II	83	. . . .
III	126	1½, 1¾
IV	118	1¾
1951: I	261	. . . .
II	256	. . . .
III	275	. . . .
IV	364	. . . .
1952: I	294	. . . .
II	503	. . . .
III	931	. . . .
IV	1,391	. . . .
1953: I	1,286	1¾, 2
II	844	2
III	512	. . . .
IV	430	. . . .
1954: I	194	2, 1¾
II	147	1¾, 1½
III	83	1½
IV	164	. . . .
1955: I	377	. . . .
II	421	1½, 1¾
III	714	1¾, 2, 2¼
IV	913	2¼, 2½
1956: I	867	2½
II	933	2½, 2¾
III	809	2¾, 3
IV	716	3
1957: I	627	. . . .
II	975	. . . .
III	970	3, 3½
IV	775	3½
1958: I	277	3, 2¾, 2¼
II	130	2¼, 1¾
III	279	1¾, 2
IV	489	2, 2½
1959: I	556	2½, 3
II	788	3, 3½
III	956	3½, 4
IV	896	4

Source: Various issues of *Federal Reserve Bulletin*.

policy, more banks find themselves more often in need of temporary accommodations at the discount window as they experience reserve drains. At such times the volume of member-bank borrowing rises. In periods of weak or declining credit demands and relatively easy monetary policy, banks individually find that reserves tend to flow to them rather than away; thus the occasion for temporary borrowing arises less frequently and the volume of member-bank borrowing declines.[11]

In the discussion of rediscounting in the United States it is common to encounter references to (a) a tradition of commercial-bank reluctance to borrow from the Federal Reserve and (b) a Federal Reserve policy of discouraging reliance on rediscounting for extended periods. Manifestly, however strong the commercial-bank tradition and however potent the Federal Reserve policy, they have not stood in the way of cyclical fluctuations in the volume of rediscounting. As the foregoing quotation shows, the Federal Reserve prefers to state that in times of monetary tightness there is a greater "need" on the part of member banks for rediscounting. Economically the more informative formulation, however, is that in times of monetary tightness it is more profitable for banks to borrow from the Federal Reserve than in other periods. And the fact that the Federal-funds rate does not rise above the discount rate suggests the further conclusion that in times of monetary tightness it is more profitable for banks to borrow from the Federal Reserve than to subject themselves to the discipline of the open market in seeking reserve accommodation. It is difficult to imagine a central-bank lending service farther removed from Bagehot's conception of the lender of last resort than the discount facility afforded by the Federal Reserve System to its member banks.

[11] Answers by the Chairman of the Board of Governors of the Federal Reserve System in United States Congress, Joint Economic Committee, *Employment, Growth, and Price Levels: Hearings,* Part 10, 86th Congress, 1st Session (Washington, D. C.: U. S. Government Printing Office, 1960), p. 3394.

IV. ALTERNATIVES

Commercial banks are the principal administrators of the payments mechanism in an advanced financial system. Performing, as commercial banks do, so vital a function in the operation of any highly developed economy, it would be idle to question the propriety of the central bank serving as lender of last resort in Bagehot's sense. Indeed Bagehot's case has taken on added strength and importance in the course of the economic and financial development that has occurred in Western countries since the publication of *Lombard Street*. What can, however, be seriously questioned is the propriety of the rediscount facility as a technique of monetary control under conditions other than those of an actual or imminent financial panic. And even with due regard to the exceptional conditions of actual or imminent financial panic, the propriety of the rediscount facility as an instrument of central banking can still be seriously questioned.

In the first place, insofar as the rediscounting facility is a means whereby commercial banks avoid reserve deficiencies at the central bank, this facility is, in fact, or else can readily be made, superfluous. Thus, in the United States, where they are subject to a legal reserve requirement, member banks may make up an actual reserve deficiency by paying an official penalty rate. Being an actual, as well as official, penalty rate, its level is always set above the rediscount rate.[12] In practice, of course, member banks strongly prefer paying the rediscount rate to paying the official penalty rate; they even prefer asset liquidation to paying the official penalty rate. Such preferences clearly demonstrate that paying the official penalty rate is indeed a measure of last resort. Thus, in permitting member banks to make up a reserve deficiency by payment of the official penalty rate, the central bank is, in effect, already performing the role of lender of last resort, not only in periods of financial panic but at all times.

[12] The penalty rate is equal to the current discount rate plus 2 per cent.

Second, in the context of an extensive Government securities market, such as that in the United States, the instrument of open-market operations enables the central bank to serve as an ever-present and potentially massive source of liquidity for the entire financial system. Hence, over and above the last-resort reserve accommodation that commercial banks can receive from the central bank at their own initiative, the tool of open-market operations imparts to the central bank the capacity to channel liquid funds to the private economy at the central bank's initiative. Clearly, the technique of open-market operations can constitute a formidable antidote to the development of financial panics.

Thus, the case for abolition of the rediscount facility seems strong in a central-banking system where provision is, or can be made, for last-resort reserve accommodation via an official penalty rate, and where open-market operations are, or can be, instituted in the context of an extensive Government securities market. The height of the penalty rate at any point of time can be set in one of two ways. One way is for the monetary authority to fix the penalty rate at a particular level that will remain constant until such time as the monetary authority sees fit to decide upon and announce a new level. This approach is illustrated by the Bank of England. Another, more novel, way is for the monetary authority to set a differential between the penalty rate and some appropriate market rate(s), and to let the penalty rate vary as it will in accordance with the variation of the appropriate market rate(s). This latter approach is illustrated by the central banks in Canada, Finland, and New Zealand.[13] Thus in Canada, the Bank of Canada instituted and publicized in November 1956 a procedure whereby the minimum lending rate to commercial banks is ¼ per cent above the average Treasury-bill tender rate.

[13] See Peter G. Fousek, *Foreign Central Banking: The Instruments of Monetary Policy* (New York: Federal Reserve Bank of New York, 1957), pp. 18-19.

Comparing the "fixed" with the "variable" penalty rate, determination of the "variable" rate appears clearly the more efficient technique of insuring that the official penalty rate will continue to be the actual penalty rate. Moreover, determination of the "variable" rate avoids the possibility of adverse announcement effects, such as public misinterpretation, confusion, or panic reaction, ensuing from a change in the "fixed" penalty rate, the timing, direction, or magnitude of which was unexpected. Hence, the technique of the "variable" rate also frees the monetary authority from the task of attempting to anticipate, and from the possible error and fear of failing to anticipate, unwanted announcement effects of a prospective change in the "fixed" penalty rate.

In the United States, as previously noted, the closest substitute for reserve accommodation from the Federal Reserve is the open market for day-to-day reserve balances at the Federal Reserve, i.e., the Federal-funds market. Accordingly, the most plausible replacement for the System's existing rediscount facility would be a scheme of last-resort reserve accommodation via a "variable" penalty rate whose level would be geared to the Federal funds rate. Not only would this scheme ensure that the official penalty rate would continue to be an actual penalty rate, but it would also mean that the Federal funds rate would be flexible in an upward, as well as downward, direction—an attribute which the Federal funds rate now lacks under conditions of monetary restraint. And, of course, once the penalty-rate scheme is in effect, the "principles of prudent discounting" currently applicable to the System's rediscount facility could be dispensed with. For the burden of prudence will have shifted from the central bank to the member banks, once reserve accommodation from the central bank at the member banks' initiative were obtainable only at an effective penalty rate. Incidentally, any inter-district differentials in Federal funds rates could be reflected in inter-district differentials of penalty rates, if the System's present regional structure were to be preserved.

What, then, are the grounds that others have presented in support of retaining the rediscount facility for the future? Such grounds certainly merit consideration before the case for abolition of the rediscount facility can be regarded as settled.

Probably the most important apparent reason for continuing the existing rediscount facility in the United States has been provided by the Federal Reserve System itself:

> The discount mechanism acts as a safety valve, providing a temporary means of adjustment to the more frequent reserve deficiencies that occur at times of pressure on reserves. Use of the safety valve, however, does not provide an escape from monetary restraint. In the first place, a higher discount rate makes member bank borrowing more expensive. Secondly, indebted banks tend to restrict credit expansion at such times and to use reserve accretions that come into their possession to repay their debts to the Reserve Banks rather than to make additional loans and investments.[14]

Interestingly, the Federal Reserve's safety-valve argument quoted above would take on greater validity and relevance under the scheme of last-resort reserve accommodation via an effective penalty rate than under the existing rediscount facility. Thus, under the scheme of last-resort reserve accommodation, the central bank would still be "providing a temporary means of adjustment to the more frequent reserve deficiencies that occur at times of pressure on reserves." Additionally, however, the presence of an effective penalty rate would make member-bank borrowing more expensive than does the existing rediscount facility: the rate charged by the central bank would at all times be above the going Federal funds rate. By the same token, the penalty rate would impel banks even more than does the existing rediscount facility to curb credit expansion at times of pressure on reserves, and to utilize their reserve accretions for reducing their indebtedness to the central bank rather than for increasing their lending activity. Hence, under the penalty-rate scheme it would be more correct to say that under the existing

[14] Board of Governors, *Annual Report for 1957*, p. 12.

rediscount mechanism that use of the safety valve of central-bank assistance at member banks' initiative "does not provide an escape from monetary restraint." Rather than being an argument for the indispensability of the existing rediscount mechanism, the safety-valve argument turns out to be a rationale for abolition of this mechanism and institution of the penalty-rate scheme in its stead.

Quite different from that of the Federal Reserve is one further argument that has been presented in favor of retaining—even enhancing—the discretionary character of the existing rediscount mechanism. According to this other argument, the opportunity for central-bank discretion afforded by the existing rediscount mechanism can be used not only to regulate member-bank indebtedness but also to control selectively member-bank lending practices.[15] Here, then, is a proposal for using the present rediscount facility as a means of selective control of the asset structure of commercial banks.

This proposal of selective lending control stands for the reverse of a penalty rate: a rate that would give incentive to member banks to borrow from the central bank. "If banks are to avail themselves of the System's discount facilities and thereby submit to the regulation of their activities, it must in some sense be profitable for them to do so."[16] Thus, the central bank would use both the carrot and the stick: member banks would be lured with the carrot of profitable borrowing into submission to the stick of selective lending control.

The carrot-and-stick proposition is a dubious one. If the purpose is selective lending control, why confine it to those banks that choose to subject themselves to it? If many banks choose to shun the discount window to avoid central-bank regulation of their lending practices, how far down shall the discount

[15] See John A. Kareken, "Federal Reserve System Discount Policy: an Appraisal," *Banca Nazionale del Lavoro*, No. 48 (March 1959), pp. 119-122. Kareken's article includes references to other articles on rediscount policy.

[16] *Ibid.*, p. 121.

rate go or how watered down shall the selective lending control be in the effort to lure more banks to the discount window?

The conclusion is clear. Neither the safety-valve argument nor the carrot-and-stick proposition provides a basis for retaining the existing rediscount mechanism in preference to last-resort reserve accommodation via a penalty rate.

V . QUALIFICATION

Having assumed throughout that the central bank is endowed with the instrument of open-market operations in the context of an extensive Government securities market, we must now turn to the case where no such market exists or where the extent of this market is too limited to render open-market operations feasible. Thus, not being endowed with the tool of open-market operations, should the central bank also be denied the discretionary role implicit in the use of nonpenal rediscounting?

Without open-market operations and without nonpenal rediscounting, conventional central banking is limited to variation of reserve requirements and moral suasion. For reasons pointed out in other chapters, both the variation of reserve requirements and moral suasion have basic limitations that hamper their use as weapons of short-term monetary policy. In adaptability to short-term changes, rediscounting is decidedly superior to either of the former two. Consequently, to deny to the central bank the exercise of nonpenal rediscounting would amount to denying it the only weapon of conventional monetary control that, in the absence of open-market operations, would give it discretionary power for contra-cyclical purposes. Thus, in response to an actual or expected decline in economic activity, the central bank might want to lower the discount rate to a subsidy level, i.e., to a level that undercuts short-term market rates. At the subsidy rate, however, the central bank might want to lend only limited amounts. It would, therefore, stipulate the duration, frequency, and magnitude of its loans to particular member banks. Hence, while the penalty-rate scheme ensures the role of the central bank as lender of last resort, it also strips the central bank of the closest substitute for the discretionary power inherent in open-market operations.

Thus, it is one thing to supplant nonpenal rediscounting with the penalty-rate scheme where the central bank can perform open-market operations as its principal technique of monetary control. It is quite another thing to institute the penalty-rate scheme in place of nonpenal rediscounting in an economy where the central bank is, in practice, even if not in law, debarred from open-market operations. In Japan, for example, the central bank is legally authorized to engage in open-market operations. In practice, however, the Japanese Government securities market has been so narrow and commercial-bank participation in it so insignificant, that the scope for open-market operations in Japanese central banking since 1945 has been plainly negligible.[17] In such a context, to have instituted a penalty-rate scheme in place of the Bank of Japan's nonpenal rediscounting would have been to deprive the monetary authority of its only weapon with discretionary power in the exercise of contra-cyclical policy.

To summarize, nonpenal rediscounting is a plausible instrument of monetary policy in the absence of open-market operations. Where, however, open-market operations are feasible, nonpenal rediscounting is—in effect—an escape mechanism for commercial banks seeking to overcome the constraint of restrictive open-market policy. Last-resort reserve accommodation via a penalty rate eliminates this escape mechanism while retaining the safety valve of central-bank lending to member banks at the latter's initiative. Thus, in monetary systems possessing the institutional setting for open-market operations, penalty-rate rediscounting enhances the effectiveness of central-bank control.

[17] See Hugh T. Patrick, "Monetary Policy in Japan's Economic Growth, 1945-1959," *Far Eastern Survey*, xxviii (May 1959), 66-67.

6

THE PERSUASIVENESS

OF MORAL SUASION

I. LOOSE CONSTRUCTION

Interpreted loosely, moral suasion is the exposition by the monetary authority of the rationale for its policy measures. So construed, moral suasion consists of oral and written statements, published reports, testimony before governmental bodies, and speeches before members of the public by officials of the monetary authority endeavoring to explain current monetary policy. It stands to reason that a public agency of the prominence and importance of the central bank will, as a matter of principle, periodically disseminate its grounds for the line of policy it pursues in any society where public discussion of governmental measures is permitted. Even where freedom of speech is suppressed, it is commonly deemed necessary by the ruling authorities to issue pronouncements that would or should enhance public comprehension—if not support—of important measures of Government control.

To be sure, the tradition of the oldest central bank—the Bank of England—has been one of secretiveness: refusal to disclose the details of, as well as the grounds for, central-bank policy.[1] This tradition, however, derives largely from the Bank of Eng-

[1] See Richard S. Sayers, *Modern Banking*, 4th Edition (Oxford: Clarendon Press, 1958), pp. 312-314.

land's past when it was a private institution with the conventional banker's obligation to his private customers. The potency of this tradition is illustrated by the fact that between 1858 and 1929 only one official statement was made by the Bank of England regarding the circumstances under which it was impelled to charge Bank Rate.[2] That statement was not made until 1910, and even then it was made, not for elucidation of any British audience, but rather in response to the extraneous event of an American Congressional inquiry, preliminary to establishment of the Federal Reserve System.

Yet the significant point about the Bank of England's distinctive tradition is that at least since 1931—when the Macmillan Committee's report was issued—the attitude of secretiveness has come in for considerable criticism as constituting obscurity that detracts from the effectiveness of central-bank policy. Moreover, in recent years the Bank itself has been breaking with this tradition; and the demands upon the Bank for further departure from the course of obscurity are likely to mount.

Due to institutional, constitutional, political, and other factors, there may always be differences in the extent to which different central banks will furnish explanations for their actions. In general, however, one may take for granted the continued future adherence to the widespread practice of periodic official exposition of the rationale for central-bank policy. In any event, since it is essentially a matter of public relations, moral suasion as loosely interpreted will not concern us further here. Accordingly, we now turn to moral suasion as strictly interpreted.

II. FEASIBILITY OF STRICT CONSTRUCTION

Construed as a technique of central-bank control, moral suasion is the exercise of central-bank pressure upon the lending activities of particular financial institutions through exhortations

[2] See Richard S. Sayers, *Central Banking After Bagehot* (Oxford: Clarendon Press, 1957), p. 60.

to these institutions. Thus, rather than being an explanation of measures carried out by the monetary authority, moral suasion in the strict sense consists of central-bank requests to particular financial institutions that they themselves voluntarily adopt certain restrictive measures. The requests may be qualitative in character, referring only to the composition of the loans and investment that the contacted financial institutions are urged to adopt. The requests may also be quantitative, indicating the aggregate amount of loans or the particular amounts of some types of loan that the contacted financial institutions are urged not to exceed.

Effectiveness of the technique of attempting central-bank control by exhortation depends on a variety of factors. The presence or absence of any of these factors may differ widely with time and place.

First and foremost among determinants of the efficacy of moral suasion is the number of institutions to be persuaded. In Canada, for instance, the commercial banking system consists of 9 chartered banks (maintaining a total of some 4,500 branches).[3] In the United States, on the other hand, there are approximately 13,000 independent commercial banks. To be suasive with 9 bank presidents is an altogether different proposition from trying to be suasive with 13,000 bank presidents. The sheer difference in numbers of banks goes a long way toward explaining why moral suasion has been much more feasible in Canada than it is in the United States.

Second, the efficacy of moral suasion depends on the expected consequences of failure to be persuaded. It is one thing if the institutions to be persuaded expect, or are led to expect, that noncompliance with the central bank's request will evoke no more than repetition of the request. It is quite another thing if

---

[3] For an informative survey of Canadian commercial and central banking, see, for example, William C. Hood, *Financing of Economic Activity in Canada*, for the Royal Commission on Canada's Economic Prospects (Ottawa: Queen's Printer, 1959), pp. 387-428.

the institutions to be persuaded expect, or are led to expect, that noncompliance may result in the denial of certain privileges (such as borrowing from the central bank) or in the enactment into law of the contents of the central bank's request. In other words, the efficacy of moral suasion is influenced by the bargaining power of the central bank vis-à-vis the institutions to be persuaded. Thus, in England, "Throughout the postwar period until 1958 the banks have been subject to official guidance in lending to their customers; the guidance has taken the form of requests, but knowledge of the statutory power of direction has been in the background. The requests inherited from the 1940s were purely qualitative, but they were stiffened in 1951, particularly by an endeavor to restrain bank lending for long-term capital purposes."[4]

This British experience apparently contrasts with the following American development, as reported by the presidents of the Federal Reserve Banks:

> A mild degree of moral suasion probably was exercised in the fall of 1950 when Board and Reserve bank officials on several occasions indicated that reserve requirements of member banks probably would be increased unless the rapid expansion of bank credit was checked and indicated to insurance companies that their practice of large-scale selling of government securities was not in the best interest of a sound economy. Also, on different occasions during the past few years, there have been references to unorthodox or particularly restrictive reserve proposals as a possible consequence of continued monetization of government securities by banking and non-banking investors, which might be considered as a form of moral suasion. Neither of these efforts, however, met with any appreciable degree of success.[5]

[4] Committee on the Working of the Monetary System (Radcliffe Committee), *Report* (London: Her Majesty's Stationery Office, 1959), p. 150.

[5] United States Congress, Joint Committee on the Economic Report, *Monetary Policy and Management of the Public Debt: Replies to Questions and Other Material for Use of the Subcommittee on General Credit Control and Debt Management,* Part 2 (Patman Committee), 82nd Congress, 2nd Session (Washington, D. C.: U. S. Government Printing Office, 1952), pp. 718-719.

Hence, in England, amid cognizance of the statutory power of direction, moral suasion took hold. In the United States, however, amid cognizance that statutory power of direction was not only absent but rather unlikely to be instituted, moral suasion was a fickle instrument.

Yet the case of contemporary Japan illustrates that the threat of statutory action is not always necessary to render moral suasion potent. Where commercial banks are heavily dependent, as they are in Japan, upon a particular privilege granted them at the discretion of the central bank, the latter's bargaining power may be strong even without resort to threats of statutory action. Thus, in the years immediately following World War II, the Bank of Japan exercised direct control over commercial-bank lending. In 1953, however, direct control was halted and supplanted by moral suasion, called *madoguchishido* (literally "guidance at the window-opening," which Japanese frequently translate as "official guidance"). As explained by an American scholar,

> Under this practice the Bank of Japan suggests borrowing quotas for each of the city banks at a small monthly meeting of the Chief of the supervisory Business Department of the Bank of Japan with the managers of the lending departments of the large city banks having head offices in Tokyo. Although there are no formal cost penalties for exceeding quotas, *madoguchishido* proved itself rather effective in implementing the 1953-4 and 1957-8 tight money policies. Evidently such results were achieved by the forcefulness of the moral suasion and pressures which appear to be important, if backstage, features of the Japanese way of carrying out policies, at least in the monetary field.[6]

One major reason for the potency of *madoguchishido* is the fact that, particularly in conditions of boom, commercial-bank borrowing from the Bank of Japan at a nonpenal discount rate is substantial. While commercial banks can draw on the central bank's rediscount facility to their own advantage, their dependence on this facility enhances the bargaining power of the cen-

6 Hugh T. Patrick, "Monetary Policy in Japan's Economic Growth, 1945-1949," *Far Eastern Review*, xxviii (May 1959), 68.

tral bank in times of strong demand for private credit. This dependence of commercial banks on the central bank helps to explain how, in Japan, statutory direct controls over bank lending could be supplanted by moral suasion without diminution of central-bank potency. Fundamentally, therefore, it is the Bank of Japan's power of nonpenal, discretionary rediscounting that makes its moral suasion tantamount to direct lending control, in practice though not in legal form.

In the United States too, as expounded in the preceding chapter, nonpenal discretionary rediscounting exists. And under the Federal Reserve Act as amended, it is the obligation of each Federal Reserve Bank to ascertain "whether undue use is being made of bank credit for the speculative carrying of or trading in securities, real estate, or commodities, or for any other purpose inconsistent with the maintenance of sound credit conditions,"[7] such a determination to serve as a basis for granting or refusing to grant rediscounting assistance. Moreover, the "undue use" of bank credit by any member bank may constitute grounds for suspending the particular bank from utilization of the credit facilities of the Federal System for a future period to be fixed by the Federal Reserve Board. Thus, the power to deny rediscounting assistance can be utilized as reinforcement for moral suasion against the "undue use" of bank credit by member banks. In practice, the conduct of bank examinations by bank-supervisory agencies has minimized the resort by the Federal Reserve to actual denial or explicit threat of denial of rediscounting assistance as a measure against the "undue use" of bank credit.

A third factor in the effectiveness of moral suasion is the nature of the occasion for the application of this tool. War or national emergency is apt to heighten the suasive power of the central bank. On the other hand, the termination of a war or of a national emergency is apt to reduce the suasive power of the

[7] *The Federal Reserve Act As Amended Through December 31, 1956* (compiled under the direction of the Board of Governors of the Federal Reserve System), Section 4, paragraph 8.

central bank. The mere presence of inflationary pressures may appear to private financial institutions as an unconvincing reason for compliance with exhortations to self-restraint. Furthermore, if some institutions comply, while others choose to follow the dictates of the market rather than of the central bank, the morale of the "patriotic" or "public-spirited" institutions may be seriously impaired by the "immorality" of their noncompliant competitors. The prospect of the competitors' expansion at the expense of the persuaded may be too much to bear for private institutions the existence of which is due to the profit motive rather than to patriotism or charitable self-denial.

A fourth factor is the duration of the period for which the moral suasion is intended. The longer the policy of self-restraint continues or is requested, the stronger the pressures that build up against it. Even a national emergency, if it goes on indefinitely, loses its hold as a reason for compliance with exhortations that are not sooner or later supplanted by more affirmative central-bank measures. Self-imposed restrictions appear increasingly arbitrary and, therefore, become increasingly unbearable as the period for which they were intended draws on.

A fifth factor is the personality of the individual(s) administering the moral suasion. As moral suasion is a form of communication between one set of individuals and another, it is conceivable that the personality or prestige of the would-be persuader will affect the suasive power of his exhortations. Thus, in the case of the Bank of Japan's monthly meetings with the managers of the lending departments of the large Tokyo city banks, the following observation has been made: "although the monthly meetings are confidential, it was commented by people both within the Bank of Japan and in the city banks concerned that the Chief of the Bank of Japan's Business Department during the 1957-58 tight money period was an extremely forthright and forceful person of high integrity, and that he was quite successful in putting pressure on uncooperative banks."[8] In general,

8 Patrick, *op. cit.*, p. 68.

it appears plausible that the personality of the would-be persuader(s) will influence the managers of those private institutions suspecting possible favoritism in the central bank's treatment of the various private institutions to be persuaded. The greater the diversity among the individual institutions to be persuaded, the wider is the scope for suspicions of favoritism. In such a context, the personality of the central bank's representative may be of some moment.

A sixth factor is the frequency with which the exhortations by the central bank change in content. Frequent alteration of the central bank's requests is apt to become increasingly onerous to the private institutions beseeched. Thus, if an exhortation for self-restraint is followed by a signal for relaxation which, in turn, is closely followed by a new exhortation for self-restraint (etc., etc.), continued compliance will tend to dwindle. In other words, moral suasion is not suited to quick reversals.

A seventh factor is the specificity of the central bank's requests. A common problem of moral suasion is the likelihood that the more detailed the exhortations, the less acceptable they are. On the other hand, the more nebulous the exhortations, the more acceptable, but also the more inconsequential, they are. Thus the specificity of the central bank's requests is, at once, both an advantage and a disadvantage. The advantage is clarity of meaning; the disadvantage is irksomeness of compliance.

III. DESIRABILITY

In view of the limitations of moral suasion implied in the foregoing exposition, the desirability of this instrument is largely a function of the alternative tools with which the central bank is endowed. If the instrument of open-market operations exists in the context of an extensive Government securities market, moral suasion, as strictly interpreted, is redundant. As a means of regulating both the volume of bank reserves and the structure of interest rates, the tool of open-market operations scores higher than moral suasion in terms of each of the factors spelled out above. Whether in adaptability to a large number of institutions, freedom from bargaining-power constraints, suitability to recurrent peacetime application, duration of use, impersonal character, reversibility of direction, or precision of pressure, open-market operations are clearly superior to moral suasion. It is noteworthy that both in Canada and in Japan, the use of moral suasion developed in conditions wherein the respective central banks could have only rather limited recourse to open-market operations; and in both countries efforts are under way to foster the development of an extensive and active Government securities market. Thus, even in monetary systems with a relatively small number of financial institutions, the preference of central banks for open-market operations is readily understandable in terms of all of the other factors that inhibit the efficacy of moral suasion.

In the United States, the use of moral suasion came to the fore in the 1928-1929 stock-market upswing. In that setting, the Federal Reserve System sought to persuade banks to curb the growth of their loans for stock-market speculation. In more recent years, as noted above, moral suasion has been used as a substitute for restrictive open-market operations that were precluded by the System's debt-monetization policy preceding the Treasury-Federal Reserve Accord of 1951.

A particularly interesting and instructive case of still more recent use of moral suasion is contained in the May 1960 address by the President of the Federal Reserve Bank of New York to the New Jersey Bankers Association. In the course of this address, reported in the nationwide financial press,[9] the New York Bank President called attention to the relatively sharp growth of long-term lending by commercial banks in immediately preceding years. He cited the instance of the large New York City banks where term loans have come to account for more than half of the outstanding volume of business loans. He commented,

[9] *Wall Street Journal,* May 20, 1960, p. 19.

"In itself, this is not necessarily questionable, and in fact the development of the term loan in the past quarter century has undoubtedly filled a real need in the field of corporate finance; but I do believe we should avoid a situation in which banks become so heavily committed in the form of longer term advances that they cannot adequately meet the legitimate short-term needs for which commercial banking characteristically provides rather unique facilities."[10] Accordingly, he suggested that commercial bankers consider the possibility of changing the term structure of their interest rates. "For example, a higher rate on term loans might help to channel such borrowing into the long-term capital market."[11]

It would be a mistake to infer from the foregoing quotations a reversion by the New York Reserve Bank to the "commercial-loan" or "real-bills" doctrine, according to which commercial banks cater to the "legitimate needs of business" by confining their lending activity to short-term, self-liquidating commercial paper for the financing of goods in process. While the "commercial-loan" or "real-bills" doctrine may have had some tenuous connection with the Federal Reserve's original use of moral suasion against bank lending for stock-market speculation in the boom of 1928-1929, American central bankers have long since abandoned this theory as a policy norm. Indeed, in his address, the New York Bank President clearly disclaimed adherence to the "real-bills" doctrine by stating "In short, I am suggesting that there must be some happy mean between the outmoded and purist concept of confining bank lending to 'self-liquidating,' 'commercial' loans, and the development of an unduly frozen position in longer term advances."[12]

10 Alfred Hayes, President of the Federal Reserve Bank of New York, "A Breathing Spell for Monetary Policy," remarks before the 57th Annual Convention of the New Jersey Bankers Association, Atlantic City, New Jersey, May 19, 1960 (mimeograph obtained from Federal Reserve Bank of New York), p. 5.

11 *Ibid.*

12 *Ibid.*

What his address does imply, however, is that the New York Bank President is using moral suasion in favor of higher long-term interest rates as a substitute for direct restrictive open-market operations in the long-term sector. For he is evidently seeking to influence the term structure of interest rates in a particular way: he is attempting to persuade bankers to consider raising long-term relative to short-term interest rates. Direct central-bank action to this end would be possible if System policy permitted open-market operations in the intermediate- and long-term sectors. By means of swapping operations, for example, the System could simultaneously sell Treasury bonds and buy Treasury bills, thereby tending to raise long-term relative to short-term interest rates without injecting excess reserves. But the System's "bills-only" policy precludes such open-market operations outside the short-term sector. Hence, the New York Bank—which, while dissenting from the "bills-only" policy, is charged with carrying it out—can do no more than use words in lieu of open-market operations in the intermediate and long-term sectors. Here then is a substitution of "open-mouth" operations for open-market operations!

In connection with the Federal Reserve's pre-Accord policy of supporting the prices of Government bonds, the Chairman and Vice-Chairman of the Federal Open Market Committee have jointly affirmed their determination not to revert to the use of moral suasion as a substitute for open-market operations. Shortly after conclusion of the Accord, they stated, "Now that the Federal Open Market Committee is not following a policy of pegging prices of Government securities, it is the general policy and practice of the System to conduct open-market operations solely on an impersonal or objective basis without attempting to influence through personal contact or other methods of moral suasion the market decisions of investors in Government securities."[13] Indeed, one of the System's objections to the pre-Accord support

---

13 Patman Committee, *op. cit.*, Part 1, p. 632.

policy was that it necessitated periodic use of moral suasion. Hence, after abandonment of the support policy, the Chairman and Vice-Chairman declared without qualification that "It is the desire of the Open Market Committee to conduct all of its open-market operations on a completely impersonal basis and without resort to moral suasion."[14] Yet, contrary to the avowed desire, the President of the Federal Reserve Bank of New York in 1960 resorted to moral suasion.

Apparently, the "period when monetary policy was paralyzed by adherence to a policy of low and pegged interest rates on government securities"[15] has been followed by a period when monetary policy is at least partially paralyzed by a "bills-only" policy, which precludes direct open-market operations—both restrictive and expansionary—in the intermediate and long-term sectors. The foregoing case of moral suasion by the President of the New York Reserve Bank is but one clear symptom of this partial paralysis of monetary policy. But while the paralysis of the pre-Accord period was not entirely of the making of the Federal Reserve System itself, the partial paralysis of the post-Accord period is emphatically of such making. Only when the self-imposed confinement of the System's open-market activity to short-term securities is removed, will it be possible to fulfill the System's own avowed desire that open-market operations be conducted without resort to moral suasion. In brief, like the "real-bills" doctrine of commercial banking, the "Treasury bills" doctrine of central banking must be abandoned before moral suasion becomes superfluous.

[14] *Ibid.*, p. 630.

[15] Assar Lindbeck, *The "New" Theory of Credit Control in the United States: An Interpretation and Elaboration* (Stockholm: Almquist & Wiksell, 1959), p. 40.

7

THE CONTRAST BETWEEN

COMMERCIAL BANKS AND

FINANCIAL INTERMEDIARIES

I. THE NEW APPROACH

In recent years, the economic role of commercial banks has become the object of widespread interest and concern in the wake of a new "theory of finance that encompasses the theory of money." In the course of development of this theory, its authors[1] have reached some far-reaching empirical, theoretical, and policy views that merit scrutiny and appraisal. Empirically, and with reference to the United States, it is averred that commercial banks have declined in economic importance relative to other

[1] John G. Gurley and Edward S. Shaw, "Financial Aspects of Economic Development," *American Economic Review,* XLV (September 1955), 515-538; Gurley and Shaw, "Financial Intermediaries and the Saving-Investment Process," *Journal of Finance,* XI (May 1956), 257-276; Gurley and Shaw, *Money in a Theory of Finance* (Washington, D. C.: The Brookings Institution, 1960). For discussion by others, see Warren L. Smith, "On the Effectiveness of Monetary Policy," *American Economic Review,* XLVI (September 1956), 600-606; S. Clark Beise, "Are Our Monetary Controls Outmoded?" *Vital Speeches,* XXIII (December 1956), 154-157; Donald K. David, *Announcement of a National Commission on Money and Credit* (New York: Committee for Economic Development, November 21, 1957), pp. 9-10; Arthur F. Burns, *Prosperity Without Inflation* (New York: Ford-

111

financial institutions[2] since the turn of the century. Theoretically, and presumably with reference to every monetary system, it is argued that the conventional dichotomy between commercial banks, as creators of loanable funds, and financial intermediaries, as brokers of loanable funds, is fallacious. Finally, with regard to policy measures, it is suggested that the institutional limitation of direct central-bank control to commercial banks is too narrow.

With reference to these far-reaching views, the present chapter re-examines the position of commercial banks vis-à-vis other financial institutions. Accordingly, the following sections are devoted, in turn, to empirical, theoretical, and policy aspects of the new approach to financial intermediaries.

II. EMPIRICAL FINDINGS

The finding that commercial banks have declined in economic importance since 1900 relative to other financial institutions is a principal result of the pioneering study of Raymond W. Goldsmith, *Financial Intermediaries in the American Economy since*

ham University Press, 1957), pp. 43-65, 81-82; "An Overdue Study" (editorial), *New York Times,* November 25, 1956, p. E8; John M. Culbertson, "Intermediaries and Monetary Theory: A Criticism of the Gurley-Shaw Theory," *American Economic Review,* xlviii (March 1958), 119-31 (followed by Gurley and Shaw's "Reply," *ibid.,* pp. 132-138); James W. Angell, "The Monetary Standard: Objectives and Limitations," *American Economic Review,* xlviii (May 1958), 76-87 (and "Discussion" by Gurley, *ibid.,* pp. 103-105); United States Congress, Senate Committee on Finance, *Investigation of the Financial Condition of the United States: Compendium,* 85th Congress, 2nd Session (Washington, D. C.: U. S. Government Printing Office, 1958), pp. 56-63, 74, 77-79, 136, 169, 177-178, 315; Warren L. Smith, "Financial Intermediaries and Monetary Controls," *Quarterly Journal of Economics,* lxxiii (November 1959), 533-553.

[2] The term "financial institutions" is used to cover all enterprises, private and public, whose assets are predominantly claims and equities: banks of all kinds, savings and loan associations, credit unions, insurance companies, corporate pension funds, dealers and brokers, finance companies, government lending institutions, and others.

1900.[3] Goldsmith finds that the share of commercial banks in the assets of all financial institutions declined from somewhat over one-half in 1900 to about one-third in 1952.[4]

(i) The relative share of commercial banks

One qualification of this result is expressed by Goldsmith himself. He notes that "the decline for commercial banks leveled off in the early thirties, and that after a temporary increase apparently due to the credit inflation of World War II, and comparable decrease afterward, their share by 1952 had not fallen below its 1933 level."[5] That is, as Table 6 indicates, the share of commercial banks in the assets of all financial institutions was virtually the same in 1952 as in 1933—about one-third.

A second qualification emerges from further examination of the data for financial institutions other than commercial banks also presented in Table 6. In 1900, financial institutions were almost entirely private.[6] By 1952, financial institutions had come to include such sizable governmental agencies as the Federal Reserve System; Government pension, retirement, and social security funds; and Government lending institutions. In principle, the Government can grow as a financial institution (or group of institutions) by its own decree, whereas private financial institutions cannot. Furthermore, Government regulation of the policies of Government financial institutions poses a distinctly different type of problem than Government regulation of private financial institutions. Thus, from the viewpoint of both economic analysis and economic policy, the growth of commercial banks

[3] A preliminary and abbreviated version of the results of this monograph appeared in Raymond W. Goldsmith, *The Share of Financial Intermediaries in National Wealth and National Assets, 1900-1949*, National Bureau of Economic Research Occasional Paper 42 (New York: 1954).

[4] Raymond W. Goldsmith, *Financial Intermediaries in the American Economy since 1900* (Princeton, New Jersey: Princeton University Press, 1958), pp. 4, 59, 75.

[5] *Ibid.*, p. 85.

[6] *Ibid.*, p. 79.

TABLE 6. *Total Assets of Commercial Banks and of Government Financial Institutions as Relative Shares*

Year	Commercial-bank assets as per cent of assets of all financial institutions (1)	Assets of government financial institutions as per cent of assets of all financial institutions (2)	Commercial-bank assets as per cent of assets of private financial institutions (3)
1900	52.8	0.0	52.8
1912	53.5	0.2	53.6
1922	48.2	6.4	51.6
1929	39.6	4.5	41.4
1933	33.5	10.2	37.3
1939	32.7	17.9	39.9
1945	39.5	26.2	53.5
1949	34.9	24.7	46.3
1952	33.9	23.9	44.5

Source: Raymond W. Goldsmith, *Financial Intermediaries in the American Economy since 1900* (Princeton, New Jersey: Princeton University Press, 1958), p. 75 for column (1) and p. 85 for column (2); column (3) was computed from pp. 73 and 85.

in relation to private financial institutions only, is at least as relevant as the growth of commercial banks in relation to all financial institutions. Segregating, then, assets of Government agencies from those of private financial institutions, we find that the share of commercial banks in the assets of private financial institutions declined from 52.8 per cent in 1900 to 44.5 in 1952—a much smaller decline than that of the share of commercial banks in the assets of private and public financial institutions combined.

As a third qualification, it should be noted that the share of commercial banks in the assets of all private financial institutions in 1952 was no lower (indeed, somewhat higher) than in 1929. Thus the decline of commercial banks relative to other private financial institutions was accomplished by 1929. Hence, alarm or concern over the relative decline of commercial banks is nearly a generation overdue, if any alarm or concern is called for.

(ii) Relative shares within commercial-bank deposits

Another aspect of the differential growth of commercial banks and of other financial institutions has not only been overlooked but covered up in the recent interpretations. As an almost inevitable result of the emphasis on the pathbreaking deviation "from conventional doctrine in regarding the banking system as one among many financial intermediaries,"[7] it has been ignored by the authors of the new approach that American commercial banking consists of two distinct types of depository operations; demand-deposit operations (or commercial banking proper) and time-deposit operations (or savings banking). In their demand-deposit operations commercial banks create money, because demand deposits circulate as a widely accepted means of payment. In their time-deposit operations commercial banks do not create money, because time deposits do not circulate as a means of payment.

Table 7 shows the growth of both types of deposits for all operating commercial banks. In 1900 the ratio of time to demand deposits was 18.4 per cent; by 1952 this ratio had risen to 36.1 per cent. Thus over the period 1900-1952 as a whole, time deposits in commercial banks grew substantially more rapidly than demand deposits. But from 1929 (when the ratio of time deposits to demand deposits was at the high level of 75.8 per cent) to 1952, time deposits slightly more than doubled, whereas demand deposits grew substantially more than fourfold. In other words, since 1929 the growth of time deposits in commercial banks has lagged behind that of demand deposits. Indeed, had the growth of time deposits since 1929 kept pace with that of demand deposits, time deposits in commercial banks would have been higher by $47.5 billion in 1952 than they actually were. A corresponding addition of $47.5 billion to the assets of commercial banks by 1952 would have raised the share of commercial-bank assets to 55.8 per cent of the assets of all private financial insti-

[7] Gurley and Shaw, "Financial Aspects of Economic Development," p. 521.

TABLE 7. *Deposits at Operating Commercial Banks*

(In millions of dollars)

Year	Total deposits (1)	Demand deposits (2)	Time deposits (3)	Ratio of time to demand deposits (per cent) (4)
1900	6,812	5,752	1,060	18.4
1912	16,000	11,201	4,799	42.8
1922	34,300	21,822	12,478	57.2
1929	44,817	25,487	19,330	75.8
1933	30,930	18,997	11,933	62.8
1939	54,524	39,213	15,311	39.0
1945	140,517	110,205	30,312	27.5
1949	133,810	97,159	36,651	37.7
1952	157,301	115,542	41,759	36.1

Source: Goldsmith, *Financial Intermediaries in the American Economy since 1900*, Table A-3.c.

tutions—a higher share than in 1900! Thus the smallness of the over-all growth of commercial banks relative to other private financial institutions since 1929 is due to the relative decline of their time-deposit business. And it is in this type of business that commercial banks are akin to other financial institutions.

(iii) Regulation of time deposits

Federal Reserve regulation seems to have contributed to the lag of time deposits in commercial banks relative to demand deposits. Among the constraints imposed on the time-deposit operations of member banks are a cash-reserve requirement against time deposits and a maximum limit on rates of interest payable on such deposits. Both constraints are determined, in accordance with statutory provisions, by the Board of Governors of the Federal Reserve System. The limit on interest rates applies not only to member banks but also to nonmember commercial banks insured by the Federal Deposit Insurance Corporation.

TABLE 8. *Cash Ratio, Total Assets, and Number of Operating Insured Mutual Savings Banks, by State, December 31, 1957*

State	Cash and balances with other banks as percentage of time deposits (1)	Total assets (in $1,000) (2)	Number of banks (3)
All states	2.9	$27,670,922	239
Connecticut	3.5	135,047	5
Indiana	8.6	61,264	4
Maine	3.4	292,344	21
Maryland	3.3	593,501	6
Massachusetts	1.5	795,392	6
New Hampshire	2.6	296,752	12
New Jersey	3.9	1,289,866	23
New York	2.8	20,672,309	128
Ohio	6.6	348,149	3
Pennsylvania	2.2	1,871,649	7
Rhode Island	2.8	427,540	7
Vermont	3.7	137,932	7
Washington	3.1	360,246	4
Wisconsin	9.6	22,657	3
Delaware, Minnesota, and Oregon*	3.4	366,274	3

*The data for these three states are combined in the F.D.I.C. tabulation.

Source: Column (1) was computed from Federal Deposit Insurance Corporation, *Assets, Liabilities, and Capital Accounts: Commercial and Mutual Savings Banks,* Report No. 48 (Washington, D. C.: December 31, 1957), pp. 58-59; columns (2) and (3), *ibid.*

What these two constraints mean for banks with high proportion of time deposits to total deposits is reflected in the behavior of banks whose operations are confined to time deposits; namely, mutual savings banks. Under existing legislation, savings banks are eligible for membership in the Federal Reserve System. Yet, of a present total of over five hundred savings banks, only three are members.[8]

Representative data on the cash assets of savings banks explain in part the all-but-unanimous refusal of these banks to join the

[8] *Federal Reserve Bulletin,* XLIV (January 1958), 41.

Federal Reserve System. Table 8 shows, by state, the number and size of all insured savings banks and the ratio of their cash plus balances with other banks to their time-deposit liabilities. The three highest ratios occur in Wisconsin (9.6 per cent), Indiana (8.6 per cent), and Ohio (6.6 per cent); in all other states the ratio is below 4 per cent.

In Wisconsin, state law applies to savings banks a minimum cash-reserve requirement of 5 per cent of deposit liabilities. In Indiana, savings banks for reasons of their own[9] seem to adhere to a 5 per cent reserve ratio of cash assets to time deposits as a practical minimum. In Ohio, state law applies to savings banks a minimum cash-reserve requirement of 4 per cent.

Of the three savings banks that are members of the Federal Reserve System, two are in Wisconsin and one is in Indiana. One factor in these locations is plain: the cash-reserve requirement for member-bank time deposits has, for the last two decades, been 5 per cent or higher, a figure matched only in Wisconsin and Indiana. This is one reason why in no other state, including Ohio, is there to be found a savings bank that is a member of the Federal Reserve System. The System's cash-reserve requirement of 5 per cent appears to exceed what most savings banks would permanently care to hold as total cash assets.

At certain times the maximum limit on rates of interest payable to holders of time deposits operates for savings banks as an additional deterrent to becoming members of the Federal Reserve System. In periods of excess demand for credit, as in the mid 1950s, savings banks may be able and willing to pay rates of interest above the maximum level set by the Federal Reserve Board. But, if they joined the System, they would be prevented

---

[9] One possible reason is a ratio of demand deposits to total deposits that is unusually high for savings banks. A second possible reason is the existence of a relatively low, state-imposed, maximum limit on the rate of interest payable to savings depositors.

from engaging in this type of competition (price competition) for savings deposits.

In sum, the net disadvantage of Federal Reserve regulation of time deposits for banks with a high ratio of time deposits to total deposits is such that virtually an entire type of financial institution eligible for System membership remains outside Federal Reserve control. It would hardly be warranted to dismiss the case of savings banks on the ground that they have declined in relative importance since 1900. To be sure, the share of mutual savings banks in the assets of all private financial institutions did drop sharply from 12.8 per cent in 1900 to 6.0 per cent in 1952.[10] On the other hand, in 1952, savings banks still had a larger volume of assets than savings and loan associations or than credit unions, investment companies, and private non-insured pension funds combined. Moreover, the very intensity of competition from other types of thrift institutions has evidently made it all the more imperative for savings banks to stay out of the Federal Reserve System.

(iv) Comparative profitability of different deposit-mix

The retrogression of time deposits in commercial banks relative to demand deposits since 1929 points to the possibility that the time-deposit operations of member banks are less profitable than their demand-deposit operations. This possibility seems to be corroborated by cross-sectional data on the average relative profitability of member banks with different ratios of time deposits to total deposits. Table 9 presents earnings and capital ratios for four size groups of member banks, each size group divided into three classes by ratios of time deposits to total deposits.

[10] Computed from Goldsmith, *Financial Intermediaries in the American Economy*, pp. 72, 85. A part, but only a part, of this relative decline is accounted for by the very high concentration of savings banks in New York and New England (as shown in Table 8), two areas whose share in the total national assets of private financial institutions has declined. *Ibid.*, pp. 119-123.

TABLE 9.

Operating Ratios of Member Banks, by Size of Bank and by Ratio of Time to Total Deposits, 1957

(Averages of individual ratios)

Size group and class of bank	Number of banks (1)	Total expenses to total earnings (2)	Net profits to total assets (3)	Net profits to capital accounts (4)	Dividends to capital accounts (5)	Capital accounts to total assets less Government securities and cash assets (6)
All groups	6,353	68.0	.65	7.9	3.1	19.8
Total deposits $2 million and under; ratio of time to total deposits:						
Under 25 per cent	575	65.7	.79	7.6	3.1	28.8
25-50 per cent	371	70.6	.70	6.9	2.4	25.0
50 per cent and over	212	73.0	.66	6.6	2.2	22.2
Total deposits $2-$5 million; ratio of time to total deposits:						
Under 25 per cent	787	63.4	.75	8.6	3.4	22.9
25-50 per cent	854	69.3	.66	7.7	2.8	21.0
50 per cent and over	502	72.3	.61	6.9	2.6	19.2
Total deposits $5-$25 million; ratio of time to total deposits:						
Under 25 per cent	622	63.7	.66	8.7	3.3	18.8
25-50 per cent	1,171	68.9	.60	8.2	3.2	16.5
50 per cent and over	513	72.6	.55	7.0	3.0	15.9
Total deposits $25 million or over; ratio of time to total deposits:						
Under 25 per cent	314	61.3	.63	8.7	3.9	15.5
25-50 per cent	354	68.9	.55	8.2	3.6	13.8
50 per cent and over	78	74.5	.48	7.7	3.5	12.0

Source: Federal Reserve Bulletin, XLIV (June 1958), 721.

The results are the following: in each size group, as the ratio of time deposits to total deposits rises, (1) the ratio of total expenses to total earnings is higher; (2) the ratio of net profits to total assets is lower; (3) the ratio of net profits to capital accounts is lower; (4) the ratio of dividends to capital accounts is lower; and (5) the ratio of capital accounts to total assets less Government securities and cash assets is lower. Thus the higher the ratio of time to total deposits, the less profitable are banks of a given size group.[11] In light of this difference in profitability, the lag of time deposits relative to demand deposits since 1929 suggests that there has been a tendency for commercial banks over the last generation to leave more and more of the thrift-account business to other institutions.

III. THEORETICAL UNDERPINNING

Conventional monetary theory distinguishes between commercial banks, on the one hand, and financial intermediaries, on the other. The basis for this distinction consists of two elements: first, the concept of money and, second, the ability to create money. The distinguishing characteristic of money is its general acceptability as a means of payment. Among private financial institutions, only commercial banks have the capacity to create money, since only the demand-deposit liabilities of commercial banks circulate as a generally accepted means of payment. On this basis, too, rests the conventional theory of government control of commercial banks through a central bank.

(i) Financial intermediaries

As a matter of choice, one may define financial intermediaries so as to encompass commercial banks as well as other financial enterprises. Thus Goldsmith defines as financial intermediaries

[11] Cf. Deane Carson, "Bank Earnings and the Competition for Savings Deposits," *Journal of Political Economy,* LXVII (December 1959), 580-588.

all financial enterprises with the very minor exceptions of holding companies and personal holding companies.[12] Financial enterprises are "all economic units—business enterprises as well as nonprofit and government organizations—that are primarily engaged in the holding of and trading in intangible assets (claims and equities)."[13] This definition clearly includes commercial banks.

Manifestly, it would be erroneous to infer from the mere fact that commercial banks can be defined as one of several variants of financial intermediaries that the same principles of control properly apply to all these variants. Indeed, Goldsmith (who is not concerned with prescription of controls) is careful to note that in his own grouping of financial intermediaries into distinct types,

> the separation of intermediaries belonging to the banking system from other depositories is made more in deference to custom than as a reflection of a genuine difference. One very important difference among the financial intermediaries in the two groups exists, but it does not separate the banking system in a broad sense from other depositories. It rather distinguishes between (1) those depositories which are able to create money (Federal Reserve Banks and checking departments of commercial banks) and which thus in their lending and investment activities are to some extent freed (not individually but as a group) from the limitation imposed by previous receipt of deposits; and (2) all other depositories, which are not able to create money and thus are limited in their lending and investment activities to the receipt of deposits and the increase in net worth.[14]

Thus it could hardly be contended that, merely because both commercial banks and other private financial enterprises can be

12 *Ibid.*, pp. 50-51.

13 *Ibid.*, p. 50. Goldsmith states parenthetically: "The slightly more descriptive designation 'financial intermediaries" is used in this study in preference to the common term 'financial institutions,' because it indicates at once their position in the process of saving and investment." *Ibid.* He does not amplify this position, nor does he anywhere in the study use the phrase "loanable funds."

14 *Ibid.*, p. 53.

defined as financial intermediaries, it necessarily follows that they are sufficiently similar from the viewpoint of central banking to require the same set of controls. As noted, the "one very important difference" which Goldsmith identifies has been generally used not only as the basis for defining private financial enterprises other than commercial banks as financial intermediaries, but also as the theoretical basis for singling out commercial banks for central-bank regulation. The problem for monetary regulation is not whether commercial banks and other financial enterprises can be subsumed under the same term (they surely can), but whether the differences between them warrant different principles of control.

(ii) Loanable funds

In the new approach to financial intermediaries, commercial banks and other private financial institutions are not only formally subsumed under the term, financial intermediaries, but are substantively considered to be similar in their role as suppliers of loanable funds. The specific nature of this similarity appears to have undergone a rather drastic change at the hands of the authors of the new approach. Yet, whether before the change or after it, the new approach rejects the notion of a fundamental dichotomy between commercial banks and other private financial institutions as suppliers of loanable funds. Let us, therefore, examine, in turn, the initial and the revised formulations of the new approach.

(a) Initial formulation. In their first formulation, the authors of the new approach acknowledge that among private financial institutions only commercial banks create money, but they emphatically deny that banks create "loanable funds."[15] Creation of "loanable funds" is "the prerogative of spending units with surpluses on income and product account."[16] The authors ex-

[15] Gurley and Shaw, "Financial Aspects of Economic Development," pp. 521-522.
[16] *Ibid.*, p. 521.

plicitly characterize both commercial banks and other financial intermediaries as "loanable-fund brokers."[17] Thus, their consideration of commercial banks as financial intermediaries derives from their conception of loanable funds. To them, "loanable funds" are "savings, in the sense of income earned and not spent on consumption, of an increase in savers' net worth and of an increase in their net financial assets."[18]

In accordance with their social-accounting conception of "loanable funds," the authors of the new approach use the concept of "savings" in an *ex post* sense. But in the conventional use of the phrase "loanable funds"—as in the loanable-funds theory of the rate of interest—the concept of savings (as well as of investment) is applied in an *ex ante* sense.[19] So used, loanable funds are coterminous with Marshall's "free or floating capital,"[20] Machlup's "money capital,"[21] Haberler's "investible funds,"[22] and—in his work of 1950—Shaw's "disposable cash."[23] The supply of loanable funds (in the conventional usage) consists of the following components: (1) planned current gross savings; (2) planned dishoardings of idle cash balances; and (3) net creation of new money.[24] (The demand for loanable funds consists of

17 *Ibid.*

18 "Reply to Culbertson," p. 135.

19 See Dennis H. Robertson, *Essays in Monetary Theory* (London: P. S. King & Son, 1940), p. 6; S. C. Tsiang, "Liquidity Preference and Loanable Funds Theories, Multiplier and Velocity Analyses: A Synthesis," *American Economic Review*, xLVI (September 1956), 540, 551.

20 Alfred Marshall, *Principles of Economics*, 8th Edition (New York: Macmillan Company, 1920), pp. 73, 412.

21 Fritz Machlup, *The Stock Market, Credit and Capital Formation* (New York: Macmillan Company, 1940), pp. 14-15.

22 Gottfried Haberler, *Prosperity and Depression*, 4th Edition (Cambridge, Mass.: Harvard University Press, 1958), pp. 289-304.

23 Edward S. Shaw, *Money, Income, and Monetary Policy* (Chicago: Richard D. Irwin, 1950), p. 297.

24 See Dennis H. Robertson, *Utility and All That* (London: Allen & Unwin, 1952), pp. 84-85; Alvin H. Hansen, "Classical, Loanable-Fund, and Keynesian Interest Theories," *Quarterly Journal of Economics*, LXV (August 1951), 429-432; Tsiang, *op. cit.*, pp. 545-52; and Warren L. Smith, "Mone-

(1) planned current gross investment and (2) demand for cash balances to hold.)[25] Since spending units make planned savings and dishoardings and since net new creation of money is performed by the central bank and the commercial banks, commercial banks are creators—and other private financial enterprises are brokers—of loanable funds in the *ex ante* sense.

While the authors of the new approach are entitled to redefine loanable funds in an *ex post* sense, they are mistaken in inferring from their new definition that commercial banks are brokers, rather than creators, of loanable funds. For, with reference to a given period, any excess of *ex post* saving over *ex ante* saving is equal to the activation of idle balances plus the net creation of new money. Thus, even with loanable funds redefined as *ex post* savings, it is still true that commercial banks can create loanable funds: their operations can make *ex post* savings exceed *ex ante* savings. In contradistinction, other private financial institutions—collectively as well as individually—can lend no more than they have received from depositors and, therefore, cannot create loanable funds either in an *ex post* sense or in an *ex ante* sense.

(b) Revised formulation. Interestingly enough, the authors of the new approach themselves appear to have abandoned their *ex post* conception of loanable funds in the more recent and definitive formulation of the new theory of finance. In the latter formulation, the new theory treats loanable funds in the *ex ante* sense. Reverting to the conventional conception of loanable funds, the new theory of finance, nonetheless, continues to aver that commercial banks and other private financial institutions are essentially alike as suppliers of loanable funds. Specifically, the new theory maintains that all financial institutions, as well

tary Theories of the Rate of Interest: A Dynamic Analysis," *Review of Economics and Statistics*, xl (February 1958), 17-20. Note Smith's statement that "the loanable funds theory relates entirely to flows of money (funds) into (supply) and out of (demand) the capital market." (*Ibid.*, p. 18.)

[25] See Robertson, *Utility and All That*, pp. 84-85.

as spending units, can create loanable funds.[26] The only acknowledged distinction between the monetary system and nonmonetary financial intermediaries is that the monetary system "is unique in being the administrator of the payments mechanism."[27]

Now what are the implications of the uniqueness of the monetary system in being the administrator of the payments mechanism? Under a rule of 100 per cent cash reserves, it would still be true that financial institutions whose deposit liabilities were widely accepted as means of payment would be engaged in administration of the payments mechanism. Operating, however, under such a rule, the private financial institutions engaged in administration of the payments mechanism would be unable to engage in the net creation of money, i.e., in increasing the supply of means of payment beyond what it would be in their absence. Hence, the capacity of commercial banks for net creation of money involves not only the acceptability of their demand-deposit liabilities as means of payment, but also operation on fractional reserves.

Although likewise operating on fractional reserves, private financial institutions other than commercial banks lack the capacity for net creation of money. Thus, because their deposit liabilities are not widely accepted as means of payment, other private financial institutions differ from commercial banks not only in respect to administration of the payments mechanism, but also in respect to creation of money and, hence, of loanable funds.

(iii) Creators and middlemen

Our reaffirmation of the conventional dichotomy between commercial banks and other private financial institutions does not necessarily imply that the former are more enterprising or in-

[26] Gurley and Shaw, *Money in a Theory of Finance*, p. 243.
[27] *Ibid.*

ventive than the latter. Commercial banks may at times be more conservative and less venturesome in their lending and investment operations than other private financial enterprises, and some or most other types of private financial enterprises may be more active or aggressive in their competitive bidding for depositors. In their time-deposit operations, where they are brokers rather than creators of loanable funds, American commercial banks have lost ground to savings and loan associations between 1945 and 1955.[28] And in the competition between demand deposits and deposits of other private financial enterprises, other types of depositories may, for short or long periods, improve the returns to depositors for parting with liquidity. They may do so by offering higher rates of interest or by other devices such as giving chocolate to depositors' children or air conditioners to new depositors.

Thus, both in lending and investment activities and in interest and promotional expenditures, other private financial enterprises may be more imaginative, inventive, and enterprising than commercial banks. Such differences, however, do not alter the substance of the conclusion that, whether under the *ex post* or the *ex ante* conception of loanable funds, commercial banks are creators, while other private financial institutions are brokers (or middlemen), of loanable funds.

IV. POLICY IMPLICATIONS

The undiscriminating claim of a decline in the relative importance of commercial banks, coupled with the concurrent interpretation of monetary controls as being confined to commercial banks, has led to drastic policy conclusions. These have

[28] See David A. Alhadeff and Charlotte P. Alhadeff, "The Struggle for Commercial Bank Savings," *Quarterly Journal of Economics*, LXXII (February 1958), 1-22.

elicited favorable attention in academic,[29] commercial banking,[30] and public circles.[31]

The first conclusion is that the influence of general monetary policy, as formulated and carried out by the central bank, has been seriously weakened by the relative growth of financial institutions that have remained free from controls imposed on commercial banks.[32] The second conclusion is a corollary of the first: because the effectiveness of general monetary policy has been substantially curtailed by its being confined to commercial banks, the time has come to institute new controls that will encompass the operations of other financial enterprises.[33] The third conclusion, less frequently stated than the first two, is that the continued restriction of central-bank regulation to commercial banks may weaken the ability of commercial banks to attract enough capital to contribute significantly to the risky ventures of future economic growth.[34] It will be useful to examine the first two conclusions jointly and thereafter to turn to the third.

(i) Control of financial intermediaries

The view that the influence of the monetary authority has been reduced by the relative growth of financial institutions other than commercial banks has two aspects: one is long-term or secular, the other is short-term or cyclical. The long-term aspect is that the rapid growth of nonbank financial institutions in the course of economic development implies that money (cur-

[29] See, for example, Angell, op. cit.

[30] See Beise, op. cit., and his comments in Investigation of the Financial Condition of the United States, pp. 168-69; and J. S. Rockefeller's comments in the latter volume, ibid., p. 315. Mr. Beise and Mr. Rockefeller are the presidents, respectively, of the Bank of America and the First National City Bank of New York, two of the three largest commercial banks in the United States.

[31] See "An Overdue Study," New York Times, November 25, 1956, p. E8.

[32] See references to Gurley and Shaw and to Smith in n. 1, this chapter.

[33] Ibid.

[34] Gurley's "Discussion," p. 105.

rency outside of banks and demand deposits) becomes a smaller proportion of total financial assets. In the long run, therefore, the velocity of circulation of money is higher than it would be without the rapid growth of nonbank financial institutions. Alternatively stated, the behavior of national income is not an adequate criterion for secular monetary expansion; the diversification demand for all types of financial assets must also be taken into account: "So short-term public debt may displace money, and debt management may displace monetary controls."[35]

One can accept the thesis that the rapid growth of nonbank financial institutions makes the velocity of circulation of money higher than it would otherwise be without inferring from this thesis that the influence of the monetary authority has declined. That the shaping of long-term monetary policy becomes increasingly complex in the course of economic development does not mean that the importance of monetary policy has to that extent diminished. On the contrary, the growing need to co-ordinate long-term monetary policy with considerations of fiscal policy and debt management adds to, rather than detracts from, the importance of a monetary policy consistent with, or conducive to, economic development.

Actually, it is the short-term or cyclical aspect of the alleged decline in the effectiveness of monetary policy that has received most of the attention in recent discussion. This is readily understandable, since the argument presented in this connection relates primarily to restrictive policy, and since it is largely as an anti-inflationary force that the potency of contra-cyclical monetary policy has been generally acknowledged. In other words, what has been commonly regarded as the most effective application of contra-cyclical monetary policy is now being challenged.[36]

The argument may be summarized as follows. The central bank controls the quantity of money by regulating the volume

[35] Gurley and Shaw, "Financial Aspects of Economic Development," p. 535.

[36] See, in particular, Smith, "On the Effectiveness of Monetary Policy."

of reserves available to commercial banks. When aggregate monetary demand threatens to become excessive, the central bank can restrict the supply of reserves. In response to their tightened reserve position, commercial banks raise credit standards for borrowers and increase interest rates on loans. Now, if commercial banks were the only source of credit available to borrowers, the restrictive monetary policy would be quite effective. However, since credit can also be obtained from other financial institutions, whose operations are not subject to quantitative control by the central bank, the efficacy of restrictive monetary policy is seriously reduced.

Further support for this argument is drawn from the existence of a large and widely distributed Government debt together with a broad and efficient market for Government securities. It is suggested that, as private demand for credit increases, financial institutions are both willing and able to liquidate their holdings of Government securities and to shift into loans. Indeed, it has been observed that even in the case of commercial banks the capacity and incentive to liquidate holdings of Government securities make it possible for them to expand loans in the face of their tightened reserve position.[37] This, as well as the similar capacity of other financial enterprises, is regarded as a large-scale sabotage of conventional monetary policy—a sabotage by means of an increased velocity of circulation of the unexpanded supply of money. The remedy for this state of affairs is held to be direct control of velocity through quantitative regulation of other financial institutions as well as of commercial banks.

So stated, the argument calls for immediate qualification.[38] If the Government securities sold by financial institutions are purchased by spending units that reduce their current expenditures in order to acquire the securities, the inflationary effect of increased loans by financial institutions would be counteracted by the deflationary effect of reduced current expenditures by buy-

37 *Ibid.*, p. 597.
38 This is recognized by Smith (*ibid.*, p. 601).

ers of Government securities. But since it seems more likely that holdings of idle balances, rather than current expenditures, will initially be reduced through the purchase of securities by spending units, this need not be a major qualification.

Another consideration, however, is of much broader significance. The large size and wide distribution of Government debt —which have given rise to the fear that restrictive monetary policy is undermined by compensating increases in velocity— augment the direct influence of the central bank on financial enterprises in general. Without growth in Government debt, conventional monetary policy is largely limited to variation of reserve requirements, rediscounting policy, and moral suasion, all of which are directly applied to commercial banks only. But with the expansion of the Government securities market to the point where it involves the great bulk of financial institutions, and with the growth of the securities portfolio of the central bank in relation to the reserve base of the money supply, open-market operations have a direct impact on the lending and investment activities of financial enterprises in general. Thus the growth in Government debt has widened the scope of direct contact between the monetary authority and the various financial institutions. It has heightened the interdependence between the various sectors of the money and capital markets, and has increased the substitutability between financial assets. In consequence, the direct effects of monetary policy on financial institutions of all types have been strengthened rather than weakened.

We now turn to the general proposition that the potency of conventionally restrictive monetary policy is seriously impaired by increases in velocity, permitting the currently restricted money supply to do much of the task that would have been performed by newly created money under an easier reserve position of commercial banks. The prime objective of restrictive monetary policy is to avert or check excess aggregate monetary demand; that is, to influence the volume of money expenditures so as to avert or arrest inflation. In principle, the volume of money expenditures can be influenced by controlling the quantity of money or its velocity or both. Any inflationary rise in velocity can be offset by a further restriction of the quantity of money. So long as the central bank has sufficient powers and resources to curtail the money supply, it will be able to offset any likely inflationary increases in velocity by correspondingly tightening commercial-bank reserves.

It may be suggested that the policy of offsetting increases in velocity is too dangerous, because it may precipitate a sharp break in business expectations with a resultant drop in aggregate business activity.[39] But this suggestion is hardly satisfactory as a basis for rejecting the policy of "offsetting." For the alternative approach would be the adoption of measures for the direct regulation of velocity. Rejection of the policy of offsetting would be warranted if it were shown that measures for the direct regulation of velocity were not only feasible but also free of the menace to business expectations which the policy of "offsetting" may entail. As the real world is riddled with "imperfections," it is not enough to demonstrate that existing monetary controls are imperfect. Before other measures are espoused, it must be shown that the present methods of control cannot be used more skillfully than they have been used in the past or that their more skillful application would be inferior to an alternative set of controls.

(ii) Control of commercial banks and adequacy of bank capital

Finally, we turn to the implications of central-bank regulation for commercial-bank capital. To recall, the theoretical basis for their regulation is that commercial banks are the only private enterprises that can create new money and, hence, can increase the supply of loanable funds. Since commercial banks are the principal administrators of the economy's payments mechanism,

[39] Cf. Smith, *ibid.*, pp. 599-600; and Angell, *op. cit.*, p. 81.

their solvency, and therefore, their capital position are matters of concern for public policy.

Commercial-bank capital has, almost in its entirety, the function of a guaranty fund against the contingency of insolvency. In seeking to be prepared for such a contingency, a commercial bank can follow either or both of two procedures: (1) it can attempt to raise capital to cover the risk involved in a particular structure of assets or (2) it can so manage the structure of its assets as to reduce the risk involved to a level consistent with its present capital.[40] The existence of alternative (2) helps to explain why commercial banking is typically not treated like a public utility with a guaranteed rate of return on capital, even though it has been subjected to strict controls, partly out of concern with solvency. In other words, since conservative management of assets has been a feasible (indeed, to many, a superior) substitute for additional capital, it has appeared quite unnecessary to provide for a particular minimum rate of return on the capital of commercial banks. On the other hand, conservative management of assets tends to conflict with a lending policy favorable to risky and venturesome investment.

An explicit inference drawn by the authors of the new approach from their empirical and theoretical analysis is that the relative retrogression of American commercial banking is partially due to "regulatory suppression of the intermediary function."[41] In their terminology the "intermediary function" or "mediation" refers to the ability of commercial banks to "buy primary securities and issue, in payment for them, deposits and currency."[42] It is abundantly clear that for them the "intermediary function" refers to lending and investment activities of commercial banks in their demand-deposit operations as well as in their time-deposit operations.

[40] See Roland I. Robinson, *The Management of Bank Funds* (New York: McGraw-Hill Book Company, 1951), pp. 409-12.

[41] Gurley and Shaw, "Financial Intermediaries and the Saving-Investment Process," p. 263.

[42] *Ibid.*, p. 262.

Interestingly enough, if, in conformance with the second section of this chapter, the concept of intermediation is confined to the time-deposit operations of commercial banks, the empirical data presented in the first section lend support to the view that the "relative retrogression in American banking seems to have resulted in part from regulatory suppression of the intermediary function." For the empirical evidence indicates (a) that it has been in their time-deposit operations, in which they are brokers rather than creators of loanable funds, that American commercial banks have been lagging over the last generation; (b) that Federal Reserve regulation places the time-deposit operations of member banks at a competitive disadvantage; and (c) that the higher the proportion of time deposits to total deposits of member banks of a given size group, the weaker the capital position of banks in that group.

Interpreted, however, in the theoretical and empirical terms of this chapter, the substance of the foregoing quotation leads to policy conclusions diametrically opposite to those now being widely disseminated. Concern over the future capacity of commercial banks to foster economic growth, combined with reaffirmation of the conventional rationale for their regulation, suggests not the extension of quantitative controls to other types of financial institutions but the freeing of time-deposit operations of commercial banks from regulatory suppression. To this latter suggestion we devote the concluding chapter.

8

THE CONTROL

OF TIME DEPOSITS

The preceding chapter served to highlight the dual character of commercial banks, whose deposit liabilities are of two distinct types: deposit liabilities widely accepted as means of payment—demand deposits—and deposit liabilities not widely accepted as means of payment—time deposits. Demand deposits being the only kind of private financial liability that serves as a means of payment, that is money, it is their demand-deposit operations that mark off commercial banks from all other private financial institutions. In view of this distinctive character of their demand-deposit operations, what should be the treatment of commercial banks' time-deposit operations by the central bank? To this problem we address this last chapter.

The specific setting for our exposition is the control of commercial-bank time deposits by the monetary authority in the United States. The underlying considerations, however, are germane to the regulation of commercial-bank time deposits generally.

Two principal instruments of control are applied by the Federal Reserve System to the time-deposit operations of commercial banks. We shall examine the case for the continued application

135

of these instruments. The first one of these, dating back to the original Federal Reserve Act, is a cash-reserve requirement against time deposits in member banks.[1] This requirement, at the level of 5 per cent of time deposits since mid-1954, is subject to variation by the Board of Governors of the Federal Reserve System between a minimum statutory level of 3 per cent and a maximum statutory level of 6 per cent of time deposits. The second instrument, in existence since the Banking Act of 1933, is the Board's statutory obligation to limit by regulation the rates of interest that may be paid by member banks on time deposits.[2] The following four sections will consider, in turn, four major arguments that have been advanced in the literature in support of central-bank control over commercial-bank time deposits.

II. THE DEFINITIONAL ARGUMENT

There seems to be a swift method of terminating any discussion of the rationale for the control of commercial-bank time deposits even before such discussion has begun. The method is to define time deposits in commercial banks as money. Manifestly, once it is assumed that commercial-bank deposits are money, the issue of central-bank control is settled. On widely accepted economic grounds, control over the supply of money in all its forms must be vested in a monetary authority. Thus, if time deposits are defined as money, not only is the issue of central-bank control settled, it does not even arise.

Although this appears to be an easy, as well as swift, way out of the discussion, it also is a faulty way out. For even if time

[1] Approximately 80 per cent of total time deposits in commercial banks were held in member banks in 1959.

[2] Since the Banking Act of 1935, the interest-rate limits set by the Board are also applicable to time deposits in nonmember commercial banks insured by the Federal Deposit Insurance Corporation. More than 99 per cent of total time deposits in commercial banks were held in insured commercial banks in 1959.

deposits in commercial banks are defined as money, the question remains whether such deposits are not more nearly similar to other financial institutions' liabilities, not defined as money, than to currency or demand deposits. Thus, from an economic—rather than semantic or legal viewpoint—the definition of commercial-bank time deposits as "money," "near-money," or "nonmoney" cannot be settled arbitrarily or as a matter of personal predilection. Rather, the definition of such deposits must itself be the result of a consideration of the economic character of these deposits in comparison with certain other deposit liabilities. And the economic character of these deposits may vary markedly from one economy to another, and even in the same economy from one period to another.

A necessary, and sufficient, condition for monetary status of a given object is that it be widely accepted as a means of payment. This condition is, in the contemporary American economy, met by currency and by demand deposits, but is not met by time deposits in commercial banks or in any other financial institution. Should a run-of-the-mill owner of a time deposit in a commercial bank seek to make payment out of his time deposit, he would find himself making the payment by means of currency or check-book money or a combination of the two. Thus, before the time-deposit owner made the payment, there would take place a conversion—in the amount to be withdrawn—from his time deposit into currency or into a demand deposit. If it were commonly possible, as it is in present-day Canada, to make payment by drawing checks against time deposits, time deposits (or that portion thereof subject to withdrawal by check) would constitute money.[3] In the contemporary United States economy,

---

[3] Some might prefer to say that Canadian saving deposits are money because they are in practice, interest-bearing demand deposits. The two formulations amount to the same result. Whether we refer to them by their legal title, savings deposits, or by the alternative designation, interest-bearing demand deposits, such Canadian deposits are money because they are widely accepted as a means of payment.

however, time deposits are not a widely accepted means of payment, and, therefore, are not money.

Yet, with reference to the United States, a considerable number of economists have, in fact, defined commercial-bank time deposits as money. Thus, in his comprehensive study, "Monetary Velocity in the United States," R. T. Selden enumerates seventeen, out of a total of thirty-eight, published income-velocity series, the authors of which included time deposits in their definition of money.[4] Selden contributes his own series, and himself defines money to include time deposits. He explains his decision as follows:

> By all odds the main issue in the definition of money for V_y [i.e., income-velocity] ratios is whether or not it should include time deposits as well as currency and demand deposits. Analytically it makes little difference how one treats time deposits. If excluded, they must be brought into the analysis as close money substitutes. One cannot ignore time deposits in any case.
>
> Empirically, however, there is a strong case for inclusion of these deposits. (1) prior to 1892 data for demand deposits alone do not exist; estimates of V_y before this date necessarily include time deposits in money. (2) The present system of differential reserve requirements for demand and time deposits at member banks did not begin until 1917. Classifications of deposits are particularly suspect for the period 1892-1917, since precise classification did not have the significance to bankers and depositors then that it has had more recently. (3) Since 1917 there have been shifts between demand and time deposits because of changes in the conditions attached to each type of deposit. The reasons for including time deposits in money are particularly compelling for study of long-run trends. Hence the analysis . . . deals exclusively with V_y measures so defined.[5]

It is noteworthy that Selden's, as well as the other economists', generic definition encompasses not only time deposits in

[4] Richard T. Selden, "Monetary Velocity in the United States," in Milton Friedman (editor), *Studies in the Quantity Theory of Money* (Chicago: University of Chicago Press, 1956), pp. 179-257.

[5] *Ibid.*, p. 237.

commercial banks, but all time deposits, including time deposits in mutual savings banks. If such a definition of money were adopted today, share accounts in savings and loan associations would, by the same token, qualify for inclusion under "money" and, therefore, under central-bank control. For share accounts in savings and loan associations are more nearly similar to time deposits in commercial and savings banks than demand deposits are to time deposits. Neither time deposits in banks nor share accounts in savings and loan associations are used as part of the circulating medium; but demand deposits are. This single ground for dichotomizing between demand deposits, on the one hand, and all other financial liabilities, on the other, is sufficient to debar the latter from monetary status.

As the above quotation from Selden points up, the case for the broader definition of money is "empirical," i.e., historical. For the study of long-term trends extending into American economic history prior to the Banking Act of 1933, the present-day clarity of the distinction between demand deposits and time deposits did not exist.

III. THE ''PRACTICAL'' ARGUMENT

Thus far we have merely observed that the acknowledged theoretical basis for the control of demand deposits does not extend to commercial-bank time deposits. From this observation we have not inferred that the existing central-bank control over commercial-bank time deposits should be removed. Such an inference would have been a *non sequitur:* from the distinctive character of demand deposits among the liabilities of private financial institutions, it does not necessarily follow that commercial-bank time deposits should be decontrolled. Granting that demand deposits must be subject to central-bank control, there may be a tenable case for concomitant control of commercial-bank time deposits, insofar as *effective* control of the former hinges upon simultaneous control of the latter. Alternatively stated, there may be *practical* reasons why it would be difficult to constrain the demand-deposit operations of commercial banks without also constraining their time-deposit operations. And indeed the literature includes important discussion in this vein.

In his *Treatise on Money*, Keynes expressed the view that there was a practical case for the control of commercial-bank time deposits. Referring to the exemption of commercial-bank deposits from a cash reserve requirement, Keynes stated,

> The practical argument against this course, and even against allowing a lower reserve ratio for deposit accounts than for current accounts, is the risk of encouraging banks to make private arrangements with, and concessions to, their customers, by which what were really Cash-deposits would masquerade as Savings-deposits, and so avoid the necessity of providing a reserve. It is stated that this evasion has in fact occurred to a certain extent in the United States.[6]

It is certainly true that during the 1920s and early 1930s, Federal Reserve authorities,[7] as well as individual scholars,[8] were calling attention to sizable evasion of the higher reserve requirement against demand deposits by means of commercial-bank inducement of customers to shift deposits from the demand to the time category. For example, according to a Federal Reserve report at the time, commercial banks in certain localities had devised a special savings account on which checks could be drawn by the depositor.[9] Concern over such practices, as re-

[6] John Maynard Keynes, *Treatise on Money* (New York: Harcourt, Brace and Company, 1930). Vol. II, pp. 13-14.

[7] See "Member Bank Reserves—Report of the Committee on Bank Reserves of the Federal Reserve System" in the Federal Reserve Board, *Annual Report for 1932* (Washington, D. C.: 1933), pp. 271-274.

[8] See Keynes's reference (*op. cit.*, p. 17) to Parker Willis, "Great Changes in American Banking," *The Banker*, May, 1927, p. 385. See also Robert G. Rodkey, *Legal Reserves in American Banking* (Ann Arbor: University of Michigan, 1934), pp. 70-71.

[9] Federal Reserve Board, *Annual Report for 1932*, pp. 272-273.

flected in the "practical" argument, gave rise to a suggestion more drastic than that of mere retention of the already existing reserve requirement against time deposits. The suggestion was that the reserve requirement against time deposits "should be fixed at the same figure named for individual demand deposits in order to eliminate the temptation for evasions."[10]

Thus, Keynes's "practical" argument was closely attuned to the contemporaneous American scene. But how valid and how relevant is this argument?

A shift in a commercial bank's deposits from the demand to the time category has two effects that work in opposite directions. On the one hand—and this is the effect stressed in the "practical" argument—such a shift provides the bank with the benefit of an increased lending capacity in consequence of the lower reserve requirement against time deposits.[11] On the other hand—and this effect is either only implied or else completely ignored in the "practical" argument—a shift of deposits confronts the bank with the cost of higher interest-rate payments on time deposits than on demand deposits.

Hence, not under all circumstances will it be profitable for a commercial bank to experience a shift of its deposits from the demand to the time category. To render such a shift profitable, the benefit to the bank from the lower reserve requirement against time deposits must not be offset by the cost to the bank from the higher interest-rate payments on these deposits.

10 Rodkey, *op. cit.*, p. 100.

11 The maximum possible expansion in the lending capacity of the entire commercial-banking system is, of course, a multiple of the increase in the lending capacity of the individual commercial bank. In the United States the individual commercial bank does not constitute the commercial-banking system. Furthermore, in the United States the monetary authority can offset any expansion in the lending capacity of the commercial-banking system deemed to be undesirable. This power of the monetary authority does not, however, detract from the "practical" argument, because that argument deals with the incentive for deposit reclassification facing the individual commercial bank. Accordingly, the analysis in the text also deals with the incentive for deposit reclassification facing the individual commercial bank.

Now during the 1920s it was, indeed, profitable for a commercial bank to induce a shift of deposits from the demand to the time category (particularly in metropolitan areas with relatively high reserve-requirement differentials as compared with country banks). Since 1933, however, the situation has been reversed: it would be clearly unprofitable for a commercial bank to induce its depositors to shift deposits from the demand to the time category.

This reversal is largely due to the fact that in the 1920s commercial banks were generally paying interest on demand deposits, whereas since 1933 this practice has been prohibited. The payment of interest on demand deposits meant that many a commercial bank found the benefit of the reserve-requirement differential to exceed the cost of the interest-rate differential. But with the effective ban of interest payment on demand deposits since 1933, a bank would have to be actively interested in renouncing profit opportunities in order to induce its customers to shift deposits from the demand to the time category. This can be made clear by the following illustration, which substantially understates the contemporary empirical situation.

Assume that commercial banks are subject to a cash-reserve requirement of 20 per cent against demand deposits, but to no reserve requirement whatever against time deposits. Also assume that commercial banks pay no interest on demand deposits, but do pay interest at 1.5 per cent per annum on time deposits. Now if a customer in a commercial bank shifted $1,000 from his demand deposit to a time deposit, the bank would have to pay him $15 in interest for the first year. On the other hand, the increase in its excess reserves—and, therefore, in its lending capacity—as a result of the deposit shift would amount to only $200. The bank would have to earn an interest rate of $\frac{15}{200} = 7.5$ per cent per annum to break even on this operation. With the likely addition of bank expenses for servicing loans, the rate of interest that would make the shift of deposits within a bank profitable to it is patently above the rates applicable to the great bulk of commercial-bank assets over the last generation, including the more recent periods of restrictive monetary policy. Since prohibition of the payment of interest on demand deposits and the subsequent proliferation of the practice of service charges on such deposits, it is no longer tempting to a commercial bank to engage in deposit reclassification.[12]

As previously noted, the foregoing illustration understated the unprofitability of deposit reclassification to a commercial bank under contemporary American conditions. The understatement was particularly significant in one respect: the assumption of no reserve requirement whatever against time deposits. This assumption was chosen so as not only to highlight actual conditions in recent years but also to illustrate the hypothetical situation of no central-bank control over commercial-bank time deposits. Thus, even with no reserve requirement against time deposits and with a reserve requirement as high as 20 per cent against demand deposits, together with an interest-rate differential of only 1.5 per cent, deposit reclassification by a commercial bank is still not rendered profitable.

What then, is the applicability and what is the validity of the "practical" argument against removal of the reserve requirement for time deposits?

Clearly since 1933 the "practical" argument has been anything but practical. Indeed, the argument would not even be practical if, as assumed in the illustration above, central-bank control over commercial-bank time deposits were removed. In

[12] That deposit reclassification is no longer profitable does not necessarily mean that commercial banks would be expected to shun all time-deposit business. The individual commercial bank "cannot allow itself to lose such deposits to its commercial-bank competitor. Not only does it earn *something* on time deposits (though perhaps very little relatively), which would then be lost, but also it would stand to lose demand deposits to the more generous and vigorously competing bank, because some bank customers like to do business with a single bank." Deane Carson, "Bank Earnings and the Competition for Savings Deposits," *Journal of Political Economy,* LXVII (December 1959), 587-588.

other words, the "practical" argument is plainly invalid. Through an appropriate exercise of central-bank control over demand deposits it is always possible to render the "practical" argument impractical, i.e., to make the reclassification of deposits unprofitable from the viewpoint of a commercial bank. First, it is possible to invoke the prohibition of interest payment on demand deposits. Next, if the first measure is not entirely adequate, it is possible to lower reserve requirements against demand deposits. The first measure or the two measures in conjunction will suffice to remove the incentive for the individual commercial bank to seek deposit reclassification.

Thus, from this point on, assume that payment of interest on demand deposits has been effectively prohibited. In that event, as already observed, so long as the interest-rate differential between time deposits and demand deposits is 1.5 percentage points or higher, the reserve-requirement differential could be as high as 20 percentage points before deposit reclassification were likely to appear attractive to a commercial bank. If the interest-rate differential were as low as 1 percentage point, a reserve-requirement differential of 13 percentage points would probably be more than adequate to render deposit reclassification by a commercial bank unprofitable. (And a reserve differential of 13 percentage points is still in excess of the present differential in the United States.) It becomes, of course, pointless to contemplate interest-rate differentials considerably below 1 per cent. Although they are entirely possible, such low differentials would reflect so clear an apathy to time deposits on the part of commercial banks, as to render any discussion of deposit reclassification under those conditions irrelevant.

It is the very relevance of the "practical" argument to the 1920s which exemplifies its invalidity as a basis for continuing the control by the central bank over commercial-bank time deposits. No sooner was payment of interest on demand deposits prohibited by the Banking Act of 1933, than the "practical" argument was rendered impractical.

Yet, ironically enough, the same Banking Act of 1933, which banned the payment of interest on demand deposits without abolishing the reserve requirement against them, also obligated the Federal Reserve Board to set limits to interest rates payable by commercial banks on time deposits. As the Board itself has noted, legislative history suggests that a primary objective of the provisions "was to prevent unsound practices in competition for time and savings deposits."[13] Thus in reacting to conditions of the 1920s, the Banking Act of 1933 reinforced Federal Reserve control over commercial-bank time deposits at the very point where one of its other provisions (the prohibition of interest payments on demand deposits) made Federal Reserve control over time deposits redundant.

The implications of this redundancy are clearly illustrated by the 1957 increase in the maximum permissible interest rate on time deposits from the 1933 level of 2.5 per cent to 3.0 per cent. In explaining its decision to raise the maximum permissible interest rates on time deposits, the Federal Reserve Board stated, "in a period of heavy demands for funds and a relatively high structure of interest rates generally, it would be desirable to permit individual member banks greater flexibility to encourage the accumulation of savings than was available under the existing maximum permissible rates. It also appeared to the Board that there was insufficient reason to prevent banks, in the exercise of management discretion, from competing actively for time and savings balances by offering rates more nearly in line with other market rates."[14] Thus, the Board itself concedes that no sooner do the limits which it has set become effective (ie., begin to hold down rates on time deposits below what they would otherwise be), than it is inclined to raise them!

One can scarcely blame the one dissenting Board member for observing, "If the ceiling should be raised whenever a few banks

13 Board of Governors of the Federal Reserve System, *Annual Report for 1956* (Washington, D. C.: 1957), p. 53.
14 *Ibid.*

feel they can afford to pay higher rates, there is no point in having a ceiling."[15] The idea needs no further belaboring: the Federal Reserve's power over interest rates on time deposits is—to apply Professor Milton Friedman's characterization of the System's existing instruments—"an accidental outgrowth of past history and by no means . . . best suited to present-day needs."[16]

IV. THE VELOCITY ARGUMENT

Over the last three decades the Federal Reserve System has published three comprehensive plans for revision of member-bank reserve requirements: in 1931, 1948, and 1959. The latter two are essentially similar in their treatment of requirements against time deposits in that both explicitly suggest that no change be made in the existing character of these requirements. Both of these plans have relatively little to say by way of explanation of their support of the *status quo*.

The full statement in the 1948 plan follows:

> There is substantial agreement that time—or at least savings —deposits should be treated separately. Such deposits are not, strictly speaking, a means of payment, but they perform other functions of money, such as being a store of value. For practical reasons the existing reserve requirements on time deposits ought to be retained as the basic requirements under the proposed plan.[17]

Enough has been said in Section II of this chapter concerning the nonmonetary nature of time deposits to require no further

[15] *Ibid.*, p. 54.

[16] Milton Friedman, "Consumer Credit Control as an Instrument of Stabilization Policy," in Board of Governors of the Federal Reserve System, *Consumer Installment Credit*, Part II, Vol. 2: *Conference on Regulation* (Washington, D. C.: 1957), p. 100.

[17] Statement of Karl R. Bopp in United States Congress, Joint Committee on the Economic Report, *Credit Policies: Hearings*, 80th Congress, 2nd Session (Washington, D. C.: U. S. Government Printing Office, 1948), p. 144.

elaboration. One could only wonder whether the unspecified "practical reasons" are anything more than the "practical" argument adduced by Keynes and others. But this will have to be left to the reader's own surmise.

Hardly more illuminating is the statement in the 1959 plan, which runs as follows:

> No change is recommended by the Board in permissible requirements against time deposits from the present range of 3 to 6 per cent. It is recognized that savings deposits in banks do not need to have as high requirements as demand deposits, which comprise the most active elements of the money supply, and the law correctly provides for differentials in such requirements. In the opinion of the Board, the present limits on requirements against time deposits are about as low as would be warranted for sound and effective operation of the banking system.[18]

In light of Section II, the present limits on requirements against time deposits appear to have imparted neither soundness nor effectiveness to the operation of the banking system.

By contrast, the 1931 plan included a scheme for a fundamental reconstitution of reserve requirements against time deposits.[19] This scheme was a logically integral part of the over-all plan, which also called for a fundamental reconstitution of reserve requirements against demand deposits. Although partly reflecting some conditions of the 1920s that have since changed radically, the plan remains a sufficiently noteworthy contribution to the subject of monetary controls to merit attention in this connection.

The 1931 plan revolved around two central themes. One was that cash-reserve requirements should be geared not only to the

[18] "Proposed Revision of Reserve Requirements," *Federal Reserve Bulletin*, xlv (April, 1959), 376.

[19] "Member Bank Reserves—Report of the Committee on Bank Reserves of the Federal Reserve System," in Federal Reserve Board, *Annual Report for 1932, op. cit.*

volume of deposits held by individual member banks but also the activity, or velocity, of these deposits. The second theme was that "member banks, because of the low reserve against time deposits, have been induced to classify as time deposits, deposits that are essentially demand in character."[20] The development of these two themes was followed by recommendations. It was recommended that the classification of deposits into time and demand should be abolished. It was further recommended that the reserve requirement against all deposits should be equivalent to a certain percentage of net deposits plus a certain percentage of the average daily debits to deposit accounts.

Although the second theme has been shown in Section III to be no longer relevant, the question remains whether deposit velocity should not serve as a criterion for reserve requirements against all deposits regardless of their formal classification. The 1931 plan argued that,

> Since the volume of member bank credit needed to meet the legitimate needs of trade and industry depends on the rate at which credit is being used as well as on its aggregate amount, it is essential for the exercise of a sound control that legal requirements differentiate in operation between highly active deposits and deposits of a less active character.[21]

What matters, therefore, is not the formal classification of deposits but their actual velocity. Accordingly, the mere fact that certain bank deposits are time deposits constitutes no ground for freeing such deposits from central-bank control.

How valid is this argument?

Manifestly, it is a truism that the impact of bank credit on the economic situation at any given time depends not only on the volume of such credit but also on the rate of its use. From this truism, however, it does not follow that member-bank reserve requirements should be made to apply to time deposits or even that reserve requirements should be geared to the rate of use of demand deposits.

20 *Ibid.*, p. 272.
21 *Ibid.*, p. 261.

So far as the idea of linking reserve requirements to the velocity of demand deposits is concerned, the 1948 plan provides some strong arguments for its rejection. In order to take into account the rate of use of demand deposits in the reserve requirements themselves,

> it would be necessary to identify either deposits or debits to deposit accounts, or both, in terms of the economic activities ... [for which the payments out of the deposits are used].... If deposits were chosen, it would be necessary to classify them, not on the basis of present ownership, but on the basis of intended expenditures—a hopeless prospect. If, on the other hand, debits were chosen, discriminatory requirements could be avoided by shifting to cash transactions, by means of "clearing arrangements," and by other devices. It is virtually impossible to devise a comprehensive system of classification which would be administratively feasible.[22]

While the foregoing feasibility objections against the velocity proposal are strong enough, they can be buttressed by a more fundamental objection. Control by the central bank over the quantity of demand deposits can, in any event, be used as counteraction to variations in deposit velocity that are deemed to be undesirable by the monetary authority. Therefore, why should a scheme of reserve requirements with weighty problems of administrative feasibility be adopted when the monetary authority already has the capacity to accomplish the avowed objective of this scheme?

Finally, regarding the application of the velocity-reserve scheme to time deposits, two points are in order. In the first place, the turnover rate of commercial-bank time deposits is but a tiny fraction of that of demand deposits. As shown in Table 10, the former rate has, in recent years, been approximately 2 per cent of the latter. By contrast, the turnover rate of commerical-bank time deposits has been very much closer to that of savings-bank deposits and savings-and-loan share accounts. Thus, if member-bank reserve requirements were geared only to the turnover rate

22 Statement by Karl R. Bopp, *op. cit.*, p. 144.

TABLE 10. *Turnover of Bank Deposits and of Share Accounts in Savings and Loan Associations in the United States*

(Times per year)

Year	Demand deposits in commercial banks	Time deposits in commercial banks	Deposits in mutual savings banks	Share accounts
1945	19.8	.50	.20	.19
1946	20.3	.60	.26	.25
1947	20.4	.56	.26	.24
1948	21.4	.51	.26	.26
1949	21.4	.45	.26	.25
1950	23.5	.48	.28	.29
1951	24.4	.46	.27	.29
1952	25.4	.46	.25	.27
1953	26.8	.46	.25	.28
1954	29.6	.46	.25	.27
1955	30.2	.47	.27	.29

Source: Economic Policy Commission, American Bankers Association, *Member Bank Reserve Requirements* (New York: 1957), p. 132.

of deposits, the inclusion or exclusion of time deposits would make so trivial a difference for the great majority of member banks, as to be hardly worth discussion. It is, therefore, quite understandable that even the 1931 plan—its references to the "considerable" turnover of commercial-bank time deposits in the 1920s notwithstanding—stipulated that the formula for member-bank reserve requirements should not be geared to deposit velocity alone. Rather, the formula was to include, in addition to the velocity consideration, the provision of a reserve equivalent to 5 per cent of all net deposits. Only by means of this provision for an undiscriminating, flat-rate treatment of demand and time deposits could the vast difference in the respective velocities of demand and time deposits be swamped in a reserve plan distinctive for its emphasis on deposit velocity!

Second, the great dissimilarity between the respective velocities of demand and time deposits is itself only a manifestation of the basic difference between the two types of deposits: a difference of kind rather than of degree. Whereas demand deposits are a widely accepted means of payment, time deposits are not. This fundamental difference did not become indubitably clear until the prohibition of interest payment on demand deposits in 1933—about two years after presentation of the velocity reserve proposal. It is to the lasting credit of this proposal that the arguments for it, as expressed in the 1931 plan, helped to bring about the 1933 clarification of the dichotomy between demand deposits and time deposits.

V. THE "VAULT-CASH" ARGUMENT

There remains one further argument against the complete removal of the cash-reserve requirement applicable to member-bank time deposits. Two features distinguish the appearance of this argument from that of the other arguments we have considered: its novelty, and its authorship. The argument in question appeared in 1957 in a detailed study, *Member Bank Reserve Requirements*, by the Economic Policy Commission of the American Bankers Association. This argument merits attention for the negative reason that it would not have been made in the first place if extensive treatment had been given in past economic literature to a basic question in this context. The question is this: how are commercial banks to administer their assets with one kind of their activity exempt, and the other kind not exempt, from central-bank control?

The first and most obvious answer is continuance of the prevailing pattern: segregation of deposits into the two major categories of demand and time, but a pooling of assets held against time deposits with assets held against demand deposits. This is the answer taken for granted in the study of the American Bankers Association.

Although it rejects the reserve requirement against member-bank time deposits as a tool of monetary control, the A.B.A. finds that "There is one valid argument *against complete exemption* of time deposits from reserve requirements."[23] This argument relates to the treatment of member banks' vault cash as part of their required reserves. Now the A.B.A. argues that if such treatment of vault cash were allowed, the exemption of time deposits from a reserve requirement "would not be completely logical."[24] For insofar as member banks maintain vault cash to meet withdrawals of time deposits, the exemption of time deposits "would give a certain amount of competitive advantage to banks having a large percentage of savings deposits."[25]

The "vault-cash" argument is a reflection of the fact that the present conduct of time-deposit operations of commercial banks is unnecessarily encumbered with central-bank control over demand-deposit operations. This argument is rendered pointless under an alternative to the prevailing administration of commercial-bank assets.

One alternative would be to permit no bank to engage both in demand-deposit and in time-deposit operations. Accordingly, commercial banks would be compelled to divest themselves of their time deposits or else become savings banks. Such a solution would be analogous to a hypothetical requirement that the thousands of American drugstores be permitted to sell only drugs, on the ground that the sale of drugs to the public must remain governmentally controlled in a manner not applicable to the sale of soft drinks or ball-point pens. This would be a clearly illogical approach. There is no more of an inherent conflict in the conduct of demand-deposit and of time-deposit operations on the same premises than there is in the selling of drugs and ball-point

23 Economic Policy Commission, American Bankers Association, *Member Bank Reserve Requirements* (New York: 1957), p. 148.
24 *Ibid.*
25 *Ibid.*

pens on the same premises. Moreover, since many customers have found it a matter of considerable convenience to patronize establishments such as commercial banks and drugstores, offering diverse products within the same walls, it would be to the distinct disadvantage of the public to have such enterprises broken up. Thus, though the exclusion of commerical banks from time-deposit operations would render the "vault-cash" argument completely impertinent, this solution does not seem to be an alternative that is preferable to the prevailing treatment of time-deposit operations.

Another alternative, however, is available. This alternative would permit commercial banks to continue their activity in time-deposit, as well as demand-deposit, operations. At the same time, this alternative would constitute full recognition of the nonmonetary character of time deposits, in line with Keynes's dictum in the *Treatise on Money* that "a system is to be welcomed which encourages as strict a segregation as possible between savings deposits and cash deposits."[26] This segregation would include not only the commonly practiced separation of time-deposit from demand-deposit liabilities, but also the separation of assets held against time-deposit liabilities from assets held against demand-deposit liabilities. Such segregation would free the time-deposit operations of commercial banks from encumbrances, such as the "vault-cash" argument, resulting from central-bank control of demand-deposit operations. Such segregation would also permit the clear and unobstructed control of demand-deposit operations by all necessary means. Instances of such segregation are readily available within the contemporary United States. In the systems of state-chartered banks of at least two states, Connecticut and Massachusetts, there is a segregation of assets, as well as liabilities, into a commercial department and a savings department. Here then is an invitation to national governments to follow the example of "segregationist" American states!

[26] Keynes, *op. cit.*, p. 17.

VI. RECAPITULATION

From none of the foregoing conclusions does it follow that the role of commercial-bank time deposits as close money substitutes ought to be ignored by the monetary authority. What these conclusions do imply is that so long as the monetary authority has control over the circulating medium, it can offset or enhance effects of the behavior of close money substitutes. Moreover, as expounded in previous chapters, freedom to operate upon the entire structure of interest rates imparts to the monetary authority the ability to offset or enhance effects of the behavior of financial claims of all maturities. Thus, while confining its direct control to commercial banks, the central bank in a monetary system with an extensive Government securities market can, through the open market, influence the activities of financial institutions generally.

INDEX

A

Alhadeff, Charlotte P., 127n.
Alhadeff, David A., 127n.
American Bankers Association, Economic Policy Commission, 46n., 151, 152
Angell, James W., 112n., 128n.
Arbitrage, 64, 65, 66
Asia, security-reserve requirements, 37n.
"Availability" doctrine, 2, 12–16

B

Bach, George L., 51n., 52n.
Bagehot, Walter, 83, 88, 91, 92
Balance of payments, 81
Bank of America, 128n.
Bank of Canada (*see also* Canada), 93
Bank of England (*see also* Bank Rate), 21:
    contrasted to Federal Reserve System, 84–88
    Discount Office, 86
    and history of central banking, 83
    and moral suasion, 99–100, 102
    penalty rate, 88, 93
    and rediscounting, 7
Bank failures, 36

Bank of Japan (*see also* Japan), 103–105
Bank Rate (*see also* Bank of England), 7, **83–98**:
    contrast with U.S. rediscount rate, 84–88
    and moral suasion, 100
    as penalty rate, 86
Banking Act of 1933, 136, 139, 144, 145
Banking Act of 1935, 136n.
Beise, S. Clark, 111n., 128n.
Belgium, security-reserve requirements in, 51n.
Bernstein, Edward M., 81n.
"Bills-only" doctrine, 5, 6, 13, 15, 30, **53–82**:
    criticism of, 69–70
    and Federal Reserve Bank of New York, 55
    "minimum intervention," 78–81
    and moral suasion, 109
    as obstruction to open-market operations, 12, 15
    rationale for, 60–70
    recession of 1958, 70–78
Bopp, Karl R., 146n., 149n.
Borrowers, 12, 27
Bronfenbrenner, Martin, 48n.
Burns, Arthur F., 111n.

155

Business cycle (*see also* Economic activity), 15, 31
Business expenditures, 69

C

Canada:
  moral suasion used in, 101, 107
  penalty rate, 93
  time deposits, 137
Carson, Deane, 121n., 143n.
Cash reserve (*see also* Cash-reserve requirements *and* Reserve requirements), excess, 12
Cash-reserve requirements (*see also* Cash reserve; Reserve requirements; *and* Security-reserve requirements), 34; *table*, 22:
  fractional, 9
  as instrument of central banking, 2
  vs. open-market operations, **19–32**
  origin of, 84
  and savings banks, 118
  vs. security reserves, 40n., 50
  set by central bank, 9
  variations in, 3, 4, 12
Central bank:
  and availability of credit, 13
  and Government debt, 11
  and interest rates, 7
  as lender of last resort, 88
  and long-term securities, 67
  purchase of bonds, 57
  and rediscounting, 7–8
  regulation of commercial banks, 9–11, 17, 18
  and reserve requirements of member banks, 3
  role of, active, 33
  separation from Treasury, 4, 50, 52
  U.S. compared with England, 21
Central Banking, 7:
  history of, 83, 84

instruments of, 2
and moral suasion, 8
theory, review of, **1–18**
Central reserve city banks, 49:
  ratio of government securities, 46
Civil War, 37n., 38
Commercial banks:
  assets, 23, 36:
    % of all financial institutions, 114; *table*, 115
  cash-reserve requirements, 40n.
  city, reserve requirements, *table*, 22
  country, reserve requirements, *table*, 22
  as creators of money, 16–18, 115, 125–27
  credit, influence on, 15
  decline in importance of, 127
  demand deposits, 40n., 115; *table*, 116
  diversity of holdings, 46
  earnings, 29, 30, 36
  earnings position *vs.* liquidity position, 41n.
  economic role of, 111–16
  extra-marginal holdings, 41–42, 44
  and financial intermediaries, 8–9:
    contrast, **111–34**
    distinction, 121, 122, 123
  and government securities, 34
  growth of, 115
  and "income" effect, 24, 25, 42, 43
  insurance against insolvency, 133
  intra-marginal holdings, 42, 47
  lending capacity, increase of, 28
  and "liquidity" effect, 24, 25, 42, 43
  and long-term securities, 67
  marginal utility, 42

and monetary policy, 1
operating ratios of, 119; *table,* 120
ratios of Government securities, 46–47
recession of 1958, 76
regulation of, by central bank, 17, 18:
  theory of, 121
reserves, excess, 24, 25, 28
retrogression, 134
security-reserve ratios, 45
shifting from government securities, 42, 43
time deposits, 115; *table,* 116:
  control of, **135–54**
total borrowing from Federal Reserve Banks, *table,* 90
Conference of University Economists, 34*n.*
Connecticut, 153:
  cash ratio and total assets of savings banks, *table,* 117
Country banks, 49:
  ratio of government securities, 46
Credit:
  availability of, 13
  control of, 12, 45
  demand for, 4, 22
  private, 3
    curbing of, 4, 27
    demand for, 23, 24, 25, 41, 42
Credit market, 32, 34:
  private, 37, 44, 86
  and yield on government debt, 51
Culbertson, John M., 58*n.*, 59*n.*, 112*n.*
Currency (*see also* Money), 17

D
David, Donald K., 111*n.*
de Chazeau, Melvin G., 35*n.*
Defense spending, 74
Deficit financing, 32, 37

Deflation, 15
Demand deposits, 9, 10, 11, 16; *table,* 22:
  in Canada, 137
  in commercial banks, 40*n.*:
    growth of, 115; *table,* 116
  compared to time deposits, 119–21; *table,* 120
  interest paid on, 142
  interest rates on, 142–145, *passim*
  regulation of, 140
  shifted to time deposits, 140–43, *passim*
  turnover, rate of, *table,* 150
  velocity of, 149, 150
Deposit liabilities, 18, 34
Deposits (*see also* Demand deposits *and* Time deposits):
  and reserve requirements, 24
  shifting of, 10
Depression, 1930's, 57, 59
Dewey, Davis R., 37*n.*
Discount rate (*see* Rediscount rate)
"Disorderly" market, 5, 6, 54, 64:
  definition of, 60–61
  in recession of 1958, 65, 70

E
Economic activity (*see also* Deflation; Inflation; *and* Business cycle), 15:
  cyclical fluctuations, 7, 12
  international, 81–82
  and monetary policy, 6
  and recession of 1958, 77
  restrictive, 21–25
  wartime, 37
Economic development projects, 32
Economic Policy Commission (*see* American Bankers Association)
Economic stability:
  and government debt, 16
  and open-market operations, **53–82**

Employment, 44, 74
England (*see also* Bank of England *and* Bank Rate), monetary system, 84*n.*
Evans, G. Heberton, Jr., viii
"Extra-marginal" holdings, 41–42, 44

F

Fand, David I., 64*n.*, 70*n.*
FDIC (*see* Federal Deposit Insurance Corporation)
Federal Deposit Insurance Corporation, 46*n.*, 47*n.*, 116, 136*n.*
Federal-funds market, 86, 87, 89, 94
Federal Reserve Act, 84:
　and moral suasion, 104
　and time deposits, 136
Federal Reserve Bank of New York, 46*n.*, 107:
　on "minimum intervention" policy, 79
　and moral suasion, 108, 110
　open-market operations, 55
　rediscount rates, *table,* 90
Federal Reserve Banks (*see also* Central bank; Federal Reserve Districts; *and* Federal Reserve System):
　moral suasion used by, 104
　and rediscounting, 7–8
　rediscount rates as penalty rates, 88
　and reserve requirements, *table,* 22
　role of, 85–86
　total member-banks' borrowing from, *table,* 90
Federal Reserve Board (*see under* Federal Reserve System)
Federal Reserve Districts, 46
Federal Reserve System (*see also* Federal Reserve Banks *and* Federal Reserve Districts):
　Ad Hoc Subcommittee on Government Securities Market, 62–65, *passim*
　"availability" doctrine, 12
　"bills-only" doctrine, 5–6, 12, 13, **53–82:**
　　criticism, 69
　Board of Governors, 20, 28, 29, 55*n.*, 60*n.*, 80*n.*, 85*n.*, 86*n.*, 87*n.*, 140*n.*
　contrasted to Bank of England, 84–88
　and interest rates, 68
　"minimum intervention" policy, 78–82
　moral suasion used by, 104
　Open Market Committee, 5, 53, 54, 55, 62, 63, 78*n.*, 80, 109, 110
　recession of 1958, 70–78
　rediscount rate, concept of, 87
　rediscounting, defense of, 95
　reserve requirements:
　　controversy, 26–28
　　revisions of, 146
　　variations in, 21
　and savings banks, 117, 118
　security-reserve requirements, objectives, 36–40
　short-term securities, 60
　and small banks, 47–48
　and stock-market speculation, 107, 108
　"swapping operation," 80–81
　time deposits, regulation of, 116–19, **135–54**
　and Treasury (*see also* Treasury-Federal Reserve Accord of 1951), 50–52
Finance, theory of, 2, 17–18, 111–34, *passim*
Financial institutions (*see also* Commercial banks; Financial intermediaries; Private financial institutions; Savings banks; *and* Savings and loan associations):

assets, % held by commercial, government, and private institutions, 113; *table,* 114
defined, 112n.
Financial intermediaries (*see also* Financial institutions *and* Private financial institutions), 3, 8–9:
and commercial banks:
contrast, **111–34**
distinction, 121, 122, 123
control of, 128–32
recession of 1958, 76
savings banks, 117, 118
theory of, 121–27
time deposits, regulation of, 116–19
Financial Intermediaries in the American Economy since 1900 (R. W. Goldsmith), 112–14
Finland, penalty rate in, 93
First National City Bank of New York, 128n.
Fiscal policies, 51
Fousek, Peter G., 38n., 51n., 93n.
Friedman, Milton, 34n., 138n., 146n.

G
Gehrels, Franz, 69n.
Gold, flow of, 32, 81, 82
Goldenweiser, Emanuel A., 35n.
Goldsmith, Raymond W., 112–14, 119n., 121, 122
Government debt:
and central bank, role of, 11
cost of, 37
and credit market, 51
dispersion of, 12
and economic stability, 16
insulation of, 4, 34n., 41
interest burden, 43
maturity distribution, 39; *table,* 39
monetization of, 36
and restrictive monetary policy, 131

servicing, 50, 52
and World War II, 33
Government expenditures, 51
Government securities (*see also* Long-term securities *and* Short-term securities):
and commercial banks, 34
compulsory holding of, 38
insulation of, 33, 42
interest rates, 37
liquidation of, by commercial banks, 30
market for, 30, 32
maturity of, *table,* 39
and Open Market Committee, 63
price support of, 14
and recession of 1958, 6, 71–73; *table,* 72; *chart,* 73
shielding of, 33
shifting from, to private loans, 13, 14, 15, 22, 24, 25, 36, 40, 43
unloading of, 4, 41
yields, 13, 71–73; *table,* 72; *chart,* 73
Gregory, Sir Theodore, 21n.
Gurley, John G., 2n., 17n., 111n., 112n., 115n., 123n., 124n., 126n., 128n., 129n., 133n.

H
Haberler, Gottfried, 124
Hansen, Alvin H., 124n.
Harris, Seymour E., 34n.
Hart, Albert G., 35n., 52n.
Hayes, Alfred, 107, 108n., 109, 110
Hicks, John R., 58n.
Hitch, Charles J., 34n.
Hood, William C., 101n.

I
"Income" effect, 24, 25, 42, 43
Indiana, cash ratio and total assets of savings banks, *table,* 117, 118
Inflation, 15, 27, 28, 41, 44, 48:

and control of money circulation, 132
and reserve-requirement variation, 21
role of commercial banks, 113
and "tight" money, 54
Interest rates:
  and "bills-only" doctrine, 64
  and central bank, 7, 10
  on demand deposits, 142–45, *passim*
  and effect on investments, 69
  and Federal Reserve System, 68
  government securities, 37
  and open-market operations, 5–6
  penalty rates, 86
  policies, flexible, 33
  and reserve requirements, 42
  structure of, 6, 14, 109
  theories of structure of, 55–60
  on time deposits, regulation of, 116, 136, 142, 145, 146
  variations in, 13
Intermediate-term securities, and open-market operations, 5–7
International economic activity, 81–82
"Intra-marginal" holdings, 42, 47
Inventory, 74, 75
Investment:
  and interest rates, 69
  and recession of 1958, 74–75, 77

J

Japan (*see also* Bank of Japan):
  monetary policies in, 98
  moral suasion used in, 103–105, 107

K

Kareken, John A., 96n.
Keynes, John Maynard, 56n., 57, 140, 147, 153
Klein, Lawrence R., 69n.
Korean War, 74
Krooss, Herman E., 37n.

L

Latin America, security requirements in, 37n.
Leith-Ross, Sir Frederick W., 38n., 51n.
Lenders, behavior of, 12, 16
Life insurance companies, and security-reserve requirements, 40
Lindbeck, Assar, 2n., 110n.
"Liquidity" effect, 24, 25, 42, 43
Loanable funds, 12, 17–18, 37n., 122n., 123–26
Loans:
  private, 4, 22
  volume of, 43
Lombard Street (Bagehot), 83, 92
London, England (*see also* Bank of England *and* England), 83, 84, 85
London Discount Market Association, 84
Long-term securities:
  interest rates, 56–60
  international aspects, 81, 82
  and moral suasion, 109
  and open-market operations, 5–7
  recession of 1958, *table,* 75
  yield changes, 13
Lutz, Friedrich A., 58n.

M

Machlup, Fritz, viii, 124
Macmillan Committee (*see under* Parliament)
Madoguchishido (Japan), 103
Maine, cash ratio and total assets of savings banks, *table,* 117
Marginal utility of bank income, 23, 24, 30, 42
Market conditions (*see* "Disorderly" market)
Marshall, Alfred, 124
Martin, William McChesney, Jr., 20, 28–29, 89, 91n.
Maryland, cash ratio and total assets of savings banks, *table,* 117

Massachusetts, 153:
  cash ratio and total assets of
    savings banks, *table,* 117
Maxwell, James G., 48*n.*
*Member Bank Reserve Require-
  ments,* 151
Mendelson, Morris, 79*n.*
Middle East, 77
Miller, Ervin, 35*n.*, 38*n.*, 49*n.*
Millikan, Max, 35*n.*
Monetary authority:
  and moral suasion, 8
  and open-market operations, 12
Monetary control:
  and "availability" doctrine, 14–
    16
  efficacy of, 11–18
  instruments of, 3
Monetary policy:
  active, 1
  anti-inflationary, 47
  contra-cyclical, 4
  and economic activity, 6
  expansionary, 3, 22, 24–25, 28,
    41
  and financial intermediaries, 128,
    129
  and fiscal policy, 48
  and moral suasion, 99–110
  "neutral," 22, 24, 41, 44, 45
  and recession, 31
  restrictive, 3, 4, 22, 23–24, 37,
    44, 129–32
  and U.S. Congress, 20*n.*
  and World War II, 33
Money (*see also* Currency):
  circulation of, 129, 132
  creation of, 16, 18, 40*n.*, 51,
    115, 121, 124
  definition of, 136–39
  theory of, 2
  and time deposits, 10, 11, 136–
    38
Money market, 21, 85
Moral suasion, 3, 8, 12, **99–110**:

by Bank of England, 99, 100,
    102, 103
in Canada, 101, 107
definition of, 99–101
desirability of, 106–110
and Federal Reserve Act, 104
and interest-rate structure, 109
in Japan, 103–105, 107
loose construction, 99–100
in national emergency, 104, 105
vs. open-market operations, 106–
    107
strict construction, 100, 106
in United States, 102, 107
Musgrave, Richard A., viii, 69*n.*

N

National Banking Act, 38
National Bureau of Economic Research, 69*n.*
New Hampshire, cash ratio and
  total assets of savings banks,
  table, 117
New Jersey, cash ratio and total
  assets of savings banks, *table,*
  117
New Jersey Bankers Association,
  107
New York, cash ratio and total assets of savings banks, *table,* 117;
  119*n.*
New York City (*see also* Federal
  Reserve Bank of New York),
  107:
  First National City Bank of,
    128*n.*
New Zealand, penalty rate in, 93

O

Ohio, cash ratio and total assets of
  savings banks, *table,* 117; 118
Open-market operations, 5–6, 7,
  53–82:
  as alternative to rediscounting,
    93
  and "bills-only" doctrine, ra-

tionale, 60–70
choice of sector, 53–55
and commercial banks, 9
exclusion of banks from, 35
expansionary, 26
and Federal Reserve System, 8
as instrument of central banking, 2
and interest rate, theories of, 55–
60
international aspect of, 81–82
"minimum intervention," 78–81
and monetary policy:
efficacy of, 11
expansionary, 44
and moral suasion, 106–107, 109
origin of, 84
in recession, 68, 70–78
and rediscount rate, 16
vs. reserve requirements, 3–4,
19–32
restrictive, 21–25, 28–31
and security-reserve operations,
49
following World War II, 33
Open-market participants, 17

P

Parliament:
Committee on the Working of
the Monetary System (Rad-
cliffe Committee), 84*n.*, 86*n.*,
102*n.*
Macmillan Committee, 100
Patman Committee (*see under*
United States Congress)
Patrick, Hugh T., 98*n.*, 103*n.*,
105*n.*
Penalty rate, 7–8, 86, 92, 93, 95,
96, 98:
Bank of England, 88
"fixed" *vs.* "variable," 94
Pennsylvania, cash ratio and total
assets of savings banks, *table*, 117
Poole, Kenyon E., 48*n.*
Private financial institutions, 3:

assets, % of all financial institutions, 113; *table*, 114
and demand deposits, 16
deposit turnover, *table*, 150
and monetary policy, 1
and reserve requirements, 20, 40
time deposits, 139
and weakness of monetary authority, 2
Production, 74
Public utilities, expenditures on, 69

R

Radcliffe Committee (*see under*
Parliament)
Recession, 31, 28, 29:
and extra-marginal holdings, 44
of 1958, 6, 62:
and "bills-only" doctrine, 70–78
"disorderly market," 65
investment in, 74–75, 77
long-term securities, *table*, 75
short-term securities, 76–77
open-market operations in, 68
Rediscounting (*see also* Rediscount
rate), 7–8:
defense of, 95
discretionary, 7
as instrument of central banking,
2
and moral suasion, 104
and penalty rate, 92, 93
revival of, in 1952, 89
and security-reserve requirements, 49
and "tight" money, 91
Rediscount rate (*see also* Bank
Rate *and* Rediscounting), 15,
83–98:
contrast with Bank Rate, 84–88
and open-market operations, 16
recession of 1958, 71, 74
role of, 87
Reserve city banks, 49
Reserve deficiency, 92
Reserve-eligible securities, 38

Reserve ratios, 21, 45
Reserve requirements (*see also* Cash-reserve requirements *and* Security-reserve requirements):
controversy, 26–28
day-to-day, 86
and deposits, 24
and penalty rate, 92, 93
% of time deposit, *table,* 117
recession of 1958, 76
revisions (1931, 1948, 1959), 146
shock effect of raising, 26, 27
and time deposits, 140–43, *passim;* 147, 151, 152
variation of *vs.* open-market operations, **19–32**
"vault-cash" requirement, 151–53
Rhode Island, cash ratio and total assets of savings banks, *table,* 117
Riefler, Winfield W., 56n., 65n., 66n., 67n., 68n.
Robertson, Dennis H., 124n., 125n.
Robinson, Roland I., 79n., 133n.
Rockefeller, James S., 128n.
Rodkey, Robert G., 140n., 141n.
Rolph, Earl R., 23n., 24n.
Roosa, Robert V., 2n., 13n., 16n., 42n., 84n.
Rosa, Robert V. (*see* Roosa, Robert V.)

S

Savers, behavior of, 12
Savings and loan associations:
security-reserve requirements, 40
share accounts, 149; *table,* 150
Savings banks:
cash ratio and total assets of, by states, *table,* 117
deposit turnover, *table,* 150
interest rates paid by, 118
and security-reserve requirements, 40
time deposits, 139

Sayers, Richard S., 19n., 20n., 21n., 26n., 83n., 99n., 100n.
Scott, Ira O., Jr., 21n., 64n., 70n.
Secondary-reserve requirements (*see* Security-reserve requirements)
Security-reserve requirements, 3, 4–5, **33–52:**
in Asia, 37n.
in Belgium, 51n.
vs. cash reserves, 50
compared with rediscounting and open-market operations, 49
desirability of, 48–52
as insulation technique, 39
and interest burden on government debt, 43
in Latin America, 37
objectives, 36–40
vs. open-market operations, **19–32**
and regional localities, 47
structure of, 45–48
timing of imposition, 41–45
in Western Europe, 38n.
Selden, R. T., 138
Seltzer, Lawrence H., 34n., 37n.
Shaw, Edward S., 2n., 17n., 111n., 112n., 115n., 123n., 124n., 126n., 128n., 129n., 133n.
Shere, Louis, 34n.
Short-term securities (*see also* Government securities *and* Long-term securities), 30, 67:
interest rates, 56–60
international aspects, 81, 82
and moral suasion, 109
and open-market operations, 5–7
and recession of 1958, 76–77
Simmons, Edward C., 36n.
Smith, Warren L., 48n., 111n., 112n., 124n., 128n., 129n., 132n.
Sproul, Allan, 79n.
Studenski, Paul, 37n.
Supplementary-reserve requirements (*see* Security-reserve re-

quirements)
"Swapping" operations, 80–81

T

Taxation, 51, 52
"Tight" money:
  and "bills-only" doctrine, 64
  and rediscounting, 91
Time deposits, 9, 10, 11; *table,* 22:
  in Canada, 137
  compared to demand deposits,
    119–21; *table,* 120
  control of, **135–54:**
    definitional argument, 136–39
    "practical" argument, 139–46
    the problem, 135–36
    "vault-cash" argument, 151–53
    velocity argument, 146–51
  defined as money, 136–38
  as demand deposits, 148, 151
  and Federal Reserve System,
    135–36
  growth of, in commercial banks,
    115–16; *table,* 116
  interest rates on, 142, 145, 146
  regulation of, 116–19
  and reserve requirements, 151
  turnover, rate of, *table,* 150
Transportation expenditures, 69
Treasury (*see also* Treasury-Federal Reserve Accord of 1951):
  and creation of money, 51
  and Federal Reserve System,
    50–52
  separation from central bank, 4
  and small banks, 48
Treasury-Federal Reserve Accord
  of 1951, 7, 37n., 54, 62, 63, 68,
  70, 107
*Treasury-Federal Reserve Study of
  the U.S. Government Securities
  Market,* 71n., 72n., 73, 75n.,
  76n., 77n.
Treatise on Money, 140, 153
Tsiang, S. C., 124n.

U

Underdeveloped economy, and se-
  curity-reserve requirements, 37
United States (*see also* Federal
  Reserve System; Government
  debt; Government securities;
  Treasury; *and* United States
  Congress):
  central banking in, 9
  moral suasion used in, 102, 107
  regulatory techniques in, 10
  security-reserve requirements, 34
United States Congress, 29n.:
  Joint Committee on the Eco-
    nomic Report, 34n., 35n., 37n.,
    49n., 62n., 102n., 146n.
  Joint Economic Committee, 54,
    61n., 69n.
  and monetary policy, 20n.
  Senate Committee on Finance,
    112n.

W

Washington, State of, cash ratio
  and total assets of savings banks,
  table, 117
Whittlesey, Charles R., 20n.
Wiggins, Suzanne, 69n.
Williams, John H., 2n.
Willis, Parker, 140n.
Wisconsin, cash ratio and total assets of savings banks, *table,* 117;
  118
World War II:
  and monetary policy, 33
  and security price support, 14
  and security-reserve require-
    ments, 34
Wright, Chester W., 37n.

Y

Yields:
  on Government securities, 71–73;
    table, 72; *chart,* 73
  on reserve securities, 43